Beating
the
Drum

How to
EXHIBIT
EFFECTIVELY
and get
better results

About the authors

David Bittleston and Martin Ralton have both had international sales and marketing careers with blue-chip companies. They formed DJB Associates in 1989 to improve their clients effectiveness at exhibitions through planning and training. They also run DJB Exhibitions which designs and builds exhibition stands for their clients with the aim of helping small companies get big.

David and Martin can be contacted at:
DJB Associates,
Pin Mill House,
Heathfield Road,
Woking,
Surrey GU22 7JJ.
Tel: 01483 723025
Fax: 01483 723221

Beating the Drum

David Bittleston and Martin Ralton

How to EXHIBIT EFFECTIVELY and get better results

Beating
the
Drum

© DJB Associates Ltd. 1995

Published by Forbes Publications
2B Drayson Mews, London W8 4LY
Tel: 0171 938 1035 Fax: 0171 938 4425

The authors have asserted their right under
the Copyright, Designs and Patents Act 1988 to be identified as Authors of this Work

Cover photos: Earls Court Olympia Ltd. Tony Anderson
The drawings in this book have been kindly supplied by Marler Haley Ltd.

Printed in Great Britain by
St Edmundsbury Press Ltd, Bury St Edmunds, Suffolk

Contents

Beating the Drum

The purpose of this book is to provide a good common sense professional approach to organising and working on your exhibition stand. Exhibitions are the greatest showcase in the world and can be the best way to expand your business, promote your service, or sell your message. Unfortunately, what is common sense to some people is a minefield of problems to others. Equally, even if we all know what should be done there are always dozens of distracting reasons that mean that deadlines are missed and ideas become jumbled. Instead of the brilliant display you had planned you end up with a hastily cobbled-together patchwork which fails to impress.

This book will help you to produce an exhibition stand that works. An exhibition stand that achieves its purpose and an exhibition stand that has appeal and interest. And , of course, the running theme throughout this book is to underline that exhibitions are a means to an end and not an end in themselves. All too often people get so involved with the details of organising and running an exhibition stand that they forget the original aims for going in the first place, if, indeed they ever had any.

Exhibitions are one of the few activities that involve the whole Marketing Mix. From market research, through new product development, through pricing, promotions and sales, and through advertising, PR and internal communications, there is something for everyone. For this reason, an exhibition can be an excellent proving ground for new and experienced marketeers alike.

So we hope that this book contains not only good solid practical advice, but also the enthusiasm and motivation to help you achieve your goals.

What is an exhibition stand?

Let's start off with a few basics. We use the term *exhibition stand* in its widest possible sense. It includes all of the following:

● A stand at a large national or international trade show.
● A stand at a regional business exhibition.
● A "Business Information Display" at a conference.
● A travelling sales "Roadshow".
● A display or presentation in a reception area.
● A stand to attract new members to your club.
● A display with public information e.g. Road Safety, or Crime Prevention.
● A stand in a shopping mall or entrance foyer.
● Open Days or Information Days at businesses or organisations.

What is the common factor in all these events? Quite simply you are there to communicate - and that communication involves selling. We must conquer that dirty S-word before it becomes a barrier.

Selling

For some people, the concept that they have something to sell is easy. Your company manufactures nuts and bolts and you go to an exhibition to sell them. Or you go to find new distributors to sell them. Or to encourage your existing customers to carry-on buying them. Or selling the idea of their great quality and reliability. Other people wrongly believe that they have nothing to sell. This is usually an excuse so that they have to do less work! But even a "message" like road safety has to be sold. (You know when people have bought it because accidents decrease.) Even "public relations" has to be sold; people have to be persuaded to "buy" your corporate message. Clubs and societies have to sell the benefits of membership, or else no-one would join. And all forms of advertising and promotion are ultimately selling the company and its products, services or messages.

So, whatever the size or venue or purpose of your exhibition stand, this book will help you make it more effective.

Is this book for you?

At one end of the scale you may be working in the Marketing Communications Department of a large international company and responsible for organising several exhibitions per year. At another end of the scale you may be a one-person company with a great idea and you need a platform from which to sell it. At another end of the scale - I never said it was linear - you may be the M.D. of an organisation who is reviewing the company exhibition strategy because there is always room for improvement. And somewhere in the middle are thousands of people who are looking for simple and effective new ideas to organise better exhibition stands.

More than 80% of all exhibitors are "small" exhibitors, but there is no rule that says they cannot make a big impact.

Of course, not everything in this book will be new or relevant to everyone. You will say "I know that", or "that's really obvious". But this is a practical guide that will help you turn all that theory into reality.

Why do so many people get it wrong?

Selling techniques are not new. Exhibitions are not new. Display techniques are not new. So why is it that I can walk round any exhibition, anywhere and see that three-quarters of all stands have got things wrong, badly wrong, or very wrong indeed? Why do companies have a desire to throw away vast sums of money? There are two possible answers:
● They don't know any better.
● They don't care.

This book is an attempt to address the former. If you fall into the latter, please send your entire exhibition budget to the authors who will make sure it goes to a worthier cause.

As we said in the introduction it is very easy to get so involved in the process of exhibiting that there is a tendency to forget why the company is there and what are the aims for attending the show. What we hope to prove in this chapter is that it is very important to have quantifiable aims for your exhibitions as it gives you a target and more importantly a method for measuring your performance.

Exhibitions offer a wide range of unique benefits over other forms of marketing and selling. In order to develop some quantifiable aims it is useful to have a look at these unique exhibition benefits.

● The customer comes to you. The visitor at an exhibition can not hide behind an officious secretary, nor is he or she in a powerful buying position. You set the scene for the business meeting.

● You can use more of the five senses. When selling an idea or a product we first have to get the customers attention. On the telephone we can only use sound. In direct mail we use only visual messages. At an exhibition we get a chance to use all five senses. In the food industry where there is a chance to get the customers to taste, touch and smell your product, you are able to get them to fully participate in the selling experience. Try and find ways of using as many of the five senses as possible on your exhibition stand.

● An opportunity to demonstrate products. Most visitors say that the main benefit to exhibitions is that you can see products being demonstrated. In this age of computers both software and hardware lend themselves to being demonstrated. Try and find ways of demonstrating your products in an interesting way.

● An exhibition gives you the opportunity to get your technical people on to the stand. Often it is too expensive to send out your technical staff to see individual customers whereas three days on an exhibition stand can be a very effective use of the technical staff's time.

● Exhibitions are a good platform for product launches. Sixty per cent or more of your audience say that the most important reason for going to an exhibition is to see what is new. If that is what they want then make sure that you always have something new to show them. Some industries even bill the exhibition with a title like "What's new in Widgets?".

● A good way to motivate the sales team. It is becoming increasingly expensive to get the sales people together. Many organisations have abandoned the annual sales conference. Therefore, exhibitions may be the only time that all the sales people get together. Used wisely, an exhibition can be partly a product training exercise, partly a sales generating exercise and partly a motivational exercise for the sales people.

● Exhibitions are a good place to meet new people. When someone changes job or moves company then it is very likely that it will be suggested they attend an exhibition to learn about the, industry, competitors, products etc. If you are looking for new customers then exhibitions are probably the quickest and easiest way of finding them.

● Senior people attend exhibitions. Our research across many industries shows that it is the senior people and the people with significant purchasing power who attend exhibitions. Of course there will also be a lot of visitors who have little or no purchasing power. The job of the stand staff is to find the right ones.

● Another big benefit of exhibitions is that you can sell new products to existing customers. In every industry getting customers is an expensive pastime. Once you have got a customer the opportunity to sell them additional products becomes very attractive. You may already be delivering to them regularly, therefore, additional sales cost very little in terms of additional transport. They already know you and they have sent up a system for paying you. Some companies shy away from inviting their existing customers on to the stand because they think that there is a possibility that they will be sold to by 'the competitors'. Apart from the opportunity of selling existing customers additional products and services, imagine how you would feel if one of your major suppliers didn't invite you to their stand and you

attended the exhibition to see them wining and dining potential customers.

● You have a chance to compete on level terms. Exhibitions give you the opportunity to make your company look bigger and more professional than it is. You can take a stand as big as the industry leader and put on a more impressive and professional display. In some industries the industry leaders have got together to control the exhibitions. They limit the size of the stands in an attempt to stop the smaller companies from increasing their market share. Fortunately, it is not just the size of the stand and the money you spend on design and build which will make you the most professional company at the exhibition.

The motivation of the visitor

When deciding what your aims are it is important to understand what the motivation of the visitor is. Increasingly people who visit exhibitions want to get something positive out of the time they give up to attend. Exhibitions are increasingly becoming an important part of the purchasing process. Our European cousins who spend more than twice what we do on exhibitions do so because exhibitions give them a really good return on their investment. In Europe exhibitions are the main forum for doing business and increasingly this is what is happening in the UK.

The visitor's motivation can be broken down into a number of key areas.

1. Having given up the time to attend they need to come away from the exhibition with something positive.

2. They are very much more open minded and willing to talk to new suppliers. This means that at an exhibition they are very much more approachable.

3. They have time. In all forms of selling you are competing for a customer's attention. Direct mail and telemarketing can sometimes fail because you are unable to control the environment. At an exhibition you have a captive audience.

4. The ability to demonstrate the product means that visitors can be given much more information in a shorter time than any other form of marketing.

Bad aims

Successful companies have clear aims about what they want to achieve, how they intend to go about it and how they are going to measure their success. We have collected a list of bad aims for attending exhibitions which include:

● *We go to exhibitions to wave the flag*
If all you want to do is wave the company flag then it is much cheaper to hire the flag poles which are situated outside the larger exhibition halls and which are normally available for hire.

● *We go because we always go*
Many companies exhibit out of habit. There is also a certain fear that if you do not attend then your customers will think that you have gone out of business. Remember that an exhibition is an opportunity for everyone to see your company. Not only do your customers see you, but your staff, your competitors and potential customers also see you. An exhibition is therefore a high risk event. If you exhibit badly then everyone sees you get it wrong. The results of exhibiting badly can be very damaging.

● *To collect as many names and addresses as possible*
At public shows where it is not possible to get a list of the names and addresses of the people who attend this can be a good aim. The problem is how many names and addresses do you want to get. An exhibition aim needs to be quantifiable. If you are attending a trade exhibition then you should be able to hire or purchase the list of people attending. This can be very much cheaper than employing stand staff to work on an exhibition stand and collect names and addresses.

● *We attend exhibitions because the staff see it as their annual perk*
If all you want to do is reward your staff for their hard work and commitment to the company then there are much cheaper ways of doing it.

● *We attend because we are the industry leaders*
Many exhibitions can only take place if the industry leaders take big stands at the front of the exhibition hall. In itself it is not a valid reason for attending. As an industry leader you should have more concrete aims for attending.

● *To answer any questions*
This response is one we usually get from people who

have not really considered why they are attending an exhibition.

Many, if not most, companies attend exhibitions for one or more of the above reasons. As exhibitions are not considered by many companies to be very important they are often given to the most junior member of the marketing team. The need to have quantifiable exhibition aims is of utmost importance. Without them there is no focus to the activity and the organising of the exhibition becomes more important than the results.

Good aims

● *To promote a new product or service*
Exhibitions are good places for new products. Most visitors who attend state that they want to see what is new. Equally, you can measure the success of doing this. How many did we sell? How many leads did we generate? How many people did we speak to about the new product?

● *To make 100 direct sales leads from the stand*
If you set out with this intention then you can measure your success at the end of the show. You can also measure the cost per sale and calculate if exhibiting is an efficient method for obtaining sales and sales leads.

● *To get 250 qualified leads*
Unlike collecting names and address, qualified leads are where your stand staff have had a conversation with a visitor and can then assess if they are a potential customer.

● *To find six new distributors*
Increasingly, with the opening up of the European market, companies are exhibiting with the aim of finding distributors who can then sell their products. At an exhibition you can find potential distributors and tell them in detail about your company. If you are trying to sell abroad then this can be a very effective way of entering the market.

● *To get written up by twenty journalists*
Most exhibitions are either organised by magazine groups or the organisers get a magazine to sponsor the event. The editors are looking for the opportunity to write about the companies that are exhibiting. They may have special previews about the exhibition and then there is normally the exhibition special, followed by the exhibition follow-up. The organiser may even let you organise a special press event at the show which can be an effective means of getting additional press coverage.

● *To launch a new corporate identity*
The image of your company sets the standard for your products, your staff, even the price you can command in the market place. You can also launch your corporate identity to the widest possible audience of existing customers, potential customers, competitors, staff, the press and everyone else who attends.

● *To be the most professional company exhibiting*
This may be a little difficult to measure. If you are the most professional you will know because everyone at the exhibition will tell you.

● *To do £20,000 worth of new business*

There are many people who will tell you that you can not sell from an exhibition stand. "Our product is too complex to sell." "It takes more than a visit to an exhibition stand to get the order" are comments that we quite often hear when asking if exhibitors can sell from their exhibition stand. I know of a number of companies who sell their products very successfully from exhibition stands. The biggest problem is getting the stand staff to ask for the order. When they achieve this you will be surprised at how many orders you can take.

Setting your exhibition aims at the start will allow you to tailor the whole of your exhibition activity.

Having fun

Should you have fun on an exhibition stand? The answer of course is yes. We all tend to take ourselves a little too seriously. A recent survey showed that 67% of professional buyers stated that the most important aspect when doing business with companies was that they liked the people. People buy people. If your stand staff are friendly and are having a good time at the exhibition then this enthusiasm will be transferred to the visitor. So look at ways of making your stand an interesting and fun place to be. Friendly, helpful people find selling easier than miserable ones.

Having listed your exhibition aims and the way in which you are going to measure your performance you are now equipped to start looking at how to go about the process.

Summary

● Before planning your exhibitions develop a list of quantifiable aims.
● Develop a list of performance measures for your exhibitions.
● People buy people. Look at ways of making your exhibition at least interesting, at best a fun packed experience.

In this section we are going to look at getting an exhibition stand from just an idea in your head to something real enough to bang your head against. We will start off with some of the fundamental considerations such as which exhibition? how big? how do I book? Then we will go on to take a closer look at the most important features of stand design and what people really notice. And, of course, we will bear in mind our running theme of "what are you trying to achieve?". All this will be affected by your biggest decision maker of all - MONEY.

Money money money

How many times have I heard people say that if they had more money they could have a better stand. Well, more money may be able to buy you a bigger stand, but remember that size isn't everything. What we should really be talking about is how you can get the best possible results from the money that you do have. Perhaps the most common mistake is for companies to spend too much money on floor space and leaving themselves with virtually nothing to spend on the things that really matter. Equally, I have never understood the wisdom where some people can spend hundreds of pounds on smart graphics, but then refuse to spend two or three pounds on some velcro tabs to hold them up. We deal with budgeting in more detail in another section, but bear in

mind that a little money can go a long way if you spend it on the right things.

Whether you have £100, £1000, or £10,000 you can make an impact and achieve your aims.

Which exhibition?

For many companies there may be only one large national exhibition per year that deals with their particular trade. If, for example, you sell air-conditioning equipment you are likely to go to the Heating and Ventilating show. If you have to promote the conference facilities in your hotel you will probably go to CONFEX, the exhibition for the conference industry.

Other companies, however, have a huge choice of shows at which to ply their wares. If you are a computer software development company you may find that you could realistically attend fifty shows per year! Past experience is always a good indicator, but before going to any show you should get the following information , usually available from the exhibition organisers.

How big is the show?
- number of exhibitors?
- total floor area in m^2
- number of visitors expected.

How much is the floor space per square metre?

Is there a profile of last year's visitors?

Is there a list or catalogue of last year's exhibitors? Were your competitors there?

Perhaps the best comparison to make between two potential shows is the cost per visitor for an imaginary 10m² stand

	SHOW A	SHOW B
Cost per 10m²	£1500	£1000
Number of visitors	10,000	5,000
Cost per visitor	15p	20p

So, show A should provide you with better value for potential sales even though it is more expensive. Ah! - if only comparisons were so simple. You may find that show B attracts 100% your target audience, whereas show A only 25% of visitors are within your target. If your calculations begin to resemble the accounts of Lloyds of London, give up and go with your gut feeling; it's as good as any other method.

Cross exhibiting

If you have the right products you should consider "cross exhibiting". This is where you can start to have interesting fun. Let's look at a few examples.

● A country hotel had been trying for months to drum up more business. Not only for its weekend trade but for midweek as well. The normal business advertising and special-offer breaks had failed to do the trick. But there is enormous competition in the hotel trade and they had to find a niche market. In an attempt to try something completely different the hotel took a stand at the "Doctors Show". (Yes, it does exist, as the General Practice Exhibition.) Here were its reasons. Doctors tend to work long hard shifts and to compensate when they have a few days off they like to get away. When the hotel took a stand at the show it was the only hotel there and so gained total attention from the visiting doctors. The results were immediate and bookings really took off.

● A supplier of office furniture found itself in the same dilemma as the hotel above. At all the normal office equipment shows this company was showing its products alongside scores of similar companies, each one trying to show its competitive edge. Although the visitor profile was good this company knew that leaving a lasting impression was difficult. A stand at the Solicitors and Legal Secretaries Exhibition seemed an odd choice at first. But why? Lawyers usually have smart offices. They need office furniture. But they are most unlikely to go to an office furniture show. The stand was so successful that the company started to go to other exhibitions aimed at professional groups.

● Lastly, the tale of a small company we have seen at several assorted shows over the last few years. They not only exhibit across different product groups, but have also crossed a consumer product into the trade arena. This company sells jacuzzi style spa baths and have been found at a bakery show, an electronic controls show and at a woodworking show. Their reasoning goes something like this: any visitor to any trade show is also a normal person with a normal life who may be a potential customer for a spa bath. That person may also relish the opportunity to look at something other than electronic controls for five minutes during the show.

Position of stand

Is the position of your stand within the exhibition hall important? Do you have a choice? It is no accident that most exhibition halls have about the same design qualities as the inside of a shoe box. The only noticeable difference is that, once inside, a shoe box is slightly more cramped. But this is only a question of relativity. Exhibition organisers will try to squeeze in as many stands as possible because that is how they make their money. If you are unfortunate, you may find yourself with a stand hidden behind a drainpipe, under the stairs, or in the corridor leading to the ladies toilets. A professional exhibitor will want to make an informed choice as to where his stand will be. However, what normally happens is that a company automatically books the same stand space as the previous year because that is what the organisers offer them. There may be better options depending on what sort of company you are and what you want to achieve.

There is only one Golden Rule: There is no "Best Position In The Hall". Your choice will be influenced by several factors.

The "Exhibition Amble"

When a visitor first enters an exhibition hall he will walk at his normal walking speed. It takes about 20 -

50 metres for him to slow down to half speed and another short distance to slow down to that wandering motion that we call the exhibition amble. It is this strange semi-conscious decrease in forward momentum that eventually causes a visitor to stop altogether; usually in the middle of the hall with a strange expression that says "Am I in the right exhibition/hall/planet and should I look at my floorplan?" Even more bizarre is the equal and opposite effect on leaving the hall. Once he has decided to leave a visitor will make a dash for the exit, with increasing speed, so that he walks out faster than he came in, despite the weight of brochures samples and leaflets.

So there you are, with your exhibition stand in a "prime position" opposite the entrance, with visitors either striding in or dashing out. Is it any wonder that they won't stop and look at your stand?. The only reason to have a stand near the entrance is if you are a large company with a well-known name and the main reason for your going to the show is to have a large corporate presence. A visitor need do no more than read your name, register that you are there and walk on. Most companies will feel that a stand in the body of the hall is more satisfactory.

Turning to the left

It is a commonly held belief that on entering an exhibition hall and presented with the choice of turning either to the left or right, about 70% of visitors will turn to the left. The reason for this is attributed to factors like because we drive on the left we are conditioned to turning left. Some people even say that it is wanting to protect the left hand side of the body. There is no real evidence that this is the case, however, if it is true then if you have a product suited to the early part of the day then it may be better to have a stand to the left of the entrance. Equally if you want to be the person who has the last word at an exhibition then being to the right of the entrance may help you achieve this. There is another school of thought that believes that everybody turns to the right because they are wearing a sword on their left hand side.

Near the facilities

Some companies believe that a stand next to the bar, snack-bar or toilets is a good idea. There is some evidence that there is slightly increased traffic flow in these positions, mainly from other exhibitors. But if you take a stand in one of these positions, don't forget to capitalise on it, i.e. don't build your stand facing the other way! One company we advised insisted that they have a stand next to the bar. As everyone who visited the exhibition was bound to visit the bar at some time during the exhibition they had plenty of seating at the front of their stand which during lunch was used by the visitors as an extension of the bar area. This made it very difficult for the stand staff to talk to the customers and they spent most of the lunch period cleaning up after the visitors had left the stand.

Perimeter site

Many visitors like to "find their bearings" in a hall and the easiest way to do this is to walk the perimeter. Psychologists might tell you that this is a primeval desire to stake-out one's territory. I say it's a desire not to get lost. Now, for some reason, perimeter sites tend to be small and undesirable. I can therefore see two advantages for taking a perimeter site:

1. You can seize the opportunity to really stand out from a long line of boring uninteresting stands.

2. A visitor who wishes to return to your stand after having done a tour of the hall may be able to locate you much more easily. A small stand in the middle of the hall will not only run the risk of being overshadowed, but may also disappear in a maze of aisles and gangways.

Centre stage

There is no doubt that most large stands will be located near the centre of the hall. The main advantages are that they can be seen from a greater distance, they have a greater pedestrian flow and that they have a greater status.. Do be wary of taking a central stand space unless you have the resources to compete on equal terms with the other large companies who will also be there. Equal terms does not mean size and money. If you are confident and assertive with your products a stand next to one of the big players can be a good way to piggy-back onto their goodwill and pulling power.

Near your competitors?

Good, positive, forward thinking companies should always want to be as close as possible to their competitors, After all, doesn't this give you the perfect opportunity to show how much better your products are? An exhibition is one of the few chances you may get to show your products on the same platform and to the same customers as your largest multi-national competitor. And remember you do not have to look big. Much more important is to look confident, look positive and look reliable. Most larger companies will rely, to a certain extent, on their long term corporate identity advertising and PR so that visitors to their stand will have a preconceived "feel good" factor about dealing with them. Your aim, as a smaller competitor, is to do everything you can on your stand to attract visitors and give them a similar comfortable feel-good factor. We discuss this more in stand design and staff attitude.

Other considerations

Some spaces have a built in opportunity for extra advertising. At Olympia and Earls Court in London, for example, a central stand gives you the ability to put up signs facing upwards. Why? Because people on the balcony can look down on your stand from above. Similarly a stand on the edge of the balcony gives you a chance to be seen from below. This is better than being in a block of stands elsewhere on the balcony.

You should also try to avoid a stand that gives onto a narrow gangway of only two metres. This is very difficult to sell from. If available, a stand opposite an open space is preferable.

Size

Once again, money will be the main deciding factor for the size of your stand-space. Anyone who tells you otherwise has probably got an after-hours job at the Royal Mint. At a large show space is typically sold at anything from £100 per square metre up to £250 per square metre depending on the popularity of the show. At those prices you will want to make the right choice. It is easy and safe to book the same size stand as your company has always had, but there many important criteria to consider. It is, of course, too obvious to say that a well presented small stand in a busy area is better than a large boring stand tucked away in a quiet corner. But first you must refer back to your aims for going to the exhibition in the first place. To talk to two thousand or more people? To make one big sale? To fly the flag? A closer look at some of the size criteria is necessary.

● **The Numbers Game**. How many visitors do you really want to visit your stand? How many do you realistically think are interested in your product? If the honest answer is only three then a large stand may serve no useful purpose at all. If on the other hand you need to speak to five hundred people to make the exhibition worthwhile then it is self-defeating to take a small stand where you can accommodate only two or three visitors: it will never be successful.

How many staff do you have available? At one extreme, two salespeople rattling around on a big stand is pointless and frustrating for a visitor. (Have you ever tried to find a salesman in a large furniture shop?) At the other extreme, too many staff on a small stand will leave no room for visitors. A bit of common sense planning should sort this one out. As a guide for smaller stands up to $24m^2$ you should allow about $3m^2$ per member of staff on the stand. For larger stands this figure can be reduced to $2m^2$ per member of staff.

If you are lucky, you may experience the "Golden Problem" that Microsoft, the computer company, recently had at an exhibition. They are aware that, as an industry leader, their stands always attract a huge number of visitors. As a result they had the largest stand at the show and had sixty salespeople available. The stand was so busy that all the staff were constantly talking to customers. Unfortunately this wasn't good enough for some visitors; Microsoft's own market research around the stand found a high level of dissatisfaction that visitors could not find a salesperson to speak to. Their solution was not to get a bigger stand at the next show, but to do larger presentations to a bigger audience and to train their staff to spend less time with each visitor.

● **Size of Competitor's Stand**. If you are the industry leader for a certain product you may think it necessary to have a larger stand than your competitors.

Conversely, if you are second or third fiddle, you may think it to be a jolly good wheeze to have a larger stand than the leader. The truth is that this will go totally unnoticed by the visitors. But it will be a major factor in the motivation of your salespeople.

At a recent exhibition in the water treatment industry, one of the product leaders decided to go 'on the cheap' and they put up their own folding-panel system inside a shell scheme. Their smaller competitors, however, had invested in a much larger space and an impressive new stand. It is doubtful whether anyone other than the two companies concerned actually noticed or cared. But the effect on the industry leader's salespeople was devastating. They became totally demoralised and honestly believed that they could not sell from an inferior stand. The company's solution was to play the size game at their next show, but they also insisted on training their salespeople better.

● **Simple Aims**. If your prime aim in going to a show is merely to reinforce your corporate identity then don't waste your money on a big stand. You are better advised to take a small stand and to spend your budget on as many poster and banner sites around the hall as you can and to do some effective PR. Visitors will assume you have a big stand there even if they failed to see you.

● **Big is Relative**. The size of your stand may depend on what you have to display. The size of the average stand at the Woodworking Machinery Exhibition is enormous. This is because the average woodworking machine is larger than the average sewing machine. In fact, last time I visited this show the average woodworking machine was larger than a fairground big dipper. However this is all nothing compared to the Printing Machinery Exhibition where some machines would not get lost in the Sahara desert.

So obviously the size of your stand is relative, not only to what you have to display, but also to the other stands around you.

● **Double-Deckers**.There is a growing fashion to build a double decker stand rather than pay for more stand space. I don't think this can be justified by cost alone. The price of putting up a large steel framework is far in excess of the extra floor space that could be bought. In addition the upstairs floor is often perceived to be out of bounds to all but the privileged few. It seems strange to alienate potential new customers in this way. Better to have more floor space and make your products more accessible to more visitors. However, a double decker can sometimes be justified from a design viewpoint; they can look fantastic.

Shape

Whereas size may not be everything, shape is certainly important. Use the analogy of your stand being a shop and the visitors are walking past your shop front. What you really want is a very long shop front, not depth. Retailers call this "foot-fall". It simply means this: if you have a stand that is open on just one side, it is better to have 8m x 2m rather

than 4m x 4m. They cost exactly the same (16 sq.m.) but one takes twice as long to walk past. Some recent research has shown that a long thin stand can achieve 50% more visitors.

Better still is a corner site with two open sides, or even a half-island site with three open sides. If you have the resources to develop it properly, an island site open on all four sides can be very effective. A stand can look much bigger than it really is. With all these stands, long and thin is better than square and deep.

Exhibition organisers do not often offer long and thin stands because they may not fit in very well with their floorplan. However, you can be creative: take three stands in a row and knock them together. Another trick is to take stands on both sides of a gangway so that visitors will have to walk *through* your stand.

Shell-scheme or space-only?

A few lines to explain exactly what we mean by these two expressions. When you book a space at an exhibition, you will probably have an option to buy one of two formats; either shell-scheme or space-only. If you buy space-only you get just what the name suggests. This is usually an area of black floor and nothing else. Nothing. No tables, no carpet , no walls, no lights. The only unexpected bonus is a free chalk mark in each corner to mark your territory. You build your own stand at the start of the show and knock it down at the end. You pay to use this space for the duration of the show, then you have to give it back. This makes it probably the most expensive leasehold property in the world.

If you buy a shell-scheme you are, in fact, buying a simple but ready-made exhibition stand. The most common type of construction is a pole and panel type, where the walls are made from large plastic panels held in an aluminium framework. Alternatively, you may find in some of the older venues a wood- construction shell-scheme which is then painted white to finish it. A simple shell-scheme package usually includes walls, carpet, ceiling structure, lights, fascia board and name board and sometimes, but only sometimes, an electric socket.

What does it cost? At a typical trade exhibition, lets say that the space-only stands are sold at £150 per square metre. So a 20m^2 stand will cost £3000. At the same show the shell scheme may sell at £180 per square metre, so the same size stand would be £3600, a difference of £600.

What are the *advantages* of a shell scheme?
● You can turn up to a ready made stand, or booth, with your name on it. You don't have to transport bulky wall panels or worry about forgetting your name.
● It is quick, easy, requires little planning and can be booked as a one stop package with your space.
● It is flexible in that you can order various extras to match, for example a cupboard, shelving, an office area, desks etc. In some cases you can specify different coloured walls

● It is also usually possible to have a variation on the theme, for example walls with no roof, or no fascia, or different coloured carpet.

Modern shell-schemes were introduced about twenty years ago and now over 65% of all exhibitors use it, proof that it has some appeal.

And the *disadvantages* of a shell scheme are:
● The main disadvantage with shell-scheme, to my mind, far outweighs all of its good points.It is you look like everyone else. It is extremely difficult to distinguish yourselves from the hundreds of other companies in similar shells around the hall.
● By their very nature they tend to be 'boxy' and square and they are not usually wide fronted.
● A shell scheme is not individual and says nothing about your company.
● The main graphic on the front of your shell is the name of your company which may be totally irrelevant to the message you are trying to put across, (see our section on graphics/ the message).
● The fascia across the front of the stand is a psychological barrier which prevents people from coming onto the stand.
● Some exhibitors choose to put their own panel system up inside a shell-scheme. This seems to be a complete waste of resources; why pay for some walls and then cover them up? A much better idea would be to pay for space-only, save £30 per square metre, hire some carpet and then put up your own system.

There are *disadvantages* of space-only:
● The main disadvantage of booking a space-only

site is that you get nothing except a patch of floor.

● The main problem for most people is that they have to do something about it some time in advance. Planning and designing takes time and cannot be left to panic management.

The *advantages* of space-only are.

● When you buy an empty space you have the opportunity to personalise it. There are many options as to what you can build in the space, which we will look at later, but the main advantage is that you can do something which gives a strong message about your company.

● You do not have to go for an expensive design and build project. The money you save from not having shell-scheme (£600 in our example above) can go a long way towards your own stand construction.

● A space-only site does not have to be a big space in the centre of the exhibition hall. It is quite normal for a space-only site to be only 4m x 3m. The smallest I have seen is only 3m x 2m. Now, the organisers may not be too keen to offer you a small space-only at first, because it is in their interests to sell as much shell-scheme as possible. But explain that what you want is a black piece of floor and take it from there.

About DIY stands

If you decide to go down the route of space-only, you can either appoint a stand contractor to design and build your stand, or if the space is small you may choose to do it yourself. Many people will remember the days of strictly controlled unionised labour within the exhibition halls. One could not so much as lift a hammer without a demand to see a union card by a chap who was always much much bigger than you. Those days are long gone. Although you are strongly advised to use an experienced contractor for large work, there is no reason why you should not lay your own carpet, paint your own walls, make your own panels, bring your own plants, or bring your own furniture. There are however two important common sense provisos to this.

1 All your work must conform to local authority and exhibition hall safety regulations. In general this means that all your constructions must be safe and made from approved materials i.e. flameproofed wood, fabrics and plastics.

2 You must use the appointed electrical contractors for all your electrical installations. Although they may be expensive, I have seen the way that most people do their own wiring when left to their own devices. The only way to ensure that the entire exhibition hall does not disappear in a puff of blue smoke is to entrust this work to qualified people.

Booking the space

At this stage you have made all the first fundamental decisions. You have researched which exhibition you want to go to, your preferred position of stand, size of stand and whether you want to book shell-scheme or space-only. Now it is time to book. The exhibition organisers will send you all the information you need and it is with them that you need to discuss all your requirements. As with all negotiations remember that nothing is ever written in tablets of stone; deals can often be done. The exhibition organisers will probably send you a contract for the space you want with demands for huge sums of money payable years in advance. In return you should receive an "Exhibitor's Manual" which will contain a vast amount of useful information about the show. The most important things you should look out for are all the other items that must be booked in advance. These are usually:

● Send plans of your proposed exhibition stand to the organisers for approval.

● Order electrical supply and sockets.

● Order furniture, flowers, carpets, telephone, water etc. where necessary.

● Send information and editorial to the organisers for your catalogue entry.

● Book hotel accommodation if required.

Of course, there are many other things to be planned in advance, depending on the complexity of your stand, but start off with the simple ones and work onwards. Do not leave things to the last minute! They will, almost inevitably, cost you more and induce severe stress disorders.

Booking late

There is a "Big Theory", often used in the holiday trade, that if you book late you can pick up some real bargains. My own experience of this is very different. I once booked late for a holiday where I had no choice of accommodation, it wasn't really cheap anyway and I ended up in a place that most smart travellers had been avoiding like the plague for years. So it is with exhibitions. It is true that there are nearly always unsold spaces at a show and you can book these right up to a few days before the start. However, there will certainly be very little choice and you will be offered a stand that no-one else wanted; probably tucked away behind the rubbish disposal. The stand may be slightly cheaper, but you do miss out on some pretty important features:

- No advance publicity
- No catalogue entry
- No chance to invite specific potential customers.

However, don't let me put you off. Many companies have had a very successful show booking merely days in advance. If you can move quickly, if you have an instant display system and you have the enthusiasm to make the most of whatever is offered, then try your luck. Even some big companies cancel their space at the last moment and you may be offered a real bargain.

Summary

- Which exhibition?
  Base your choice on the cost per target customer at each potential exhibition.
- Position of stand
  Avoid the entrance as it is difficult to get people to stop when entering or leaving the show.
  Should you choose a perimeter site?
  Should you be centre stage?
  Do you want to be near your competitor's?
- Size of stand?
  Allow $3m^2$ per stand staff.
  The size should be based on your aims and not on your budget.
  What is the size of your competitors stand.
- Shape of stand
  Remember you are buying a shop front not a warehouse.
- Shell scheme or space only
  The choice is not only about cost but also about your desire to create something that will stand out and be noticed.
- Booking the space
  You may be able to book late and save some money.

4.

In the next two sections of the book we look at the main elements to be considered when thinking about the actual layout and format for your stand. There are two main topics; to think about: stand design and graphics (*see* next section, p.32). The latter element is by far the most important because it deals with first impressions. And we all know how important it is to get those right.

The subject of stand design is complex and can never be fully covered by text alone. If you were to walk around a dozen exhibitions making a conscious effort to analyse the various designs and styles you might just begin to find a few common themes. But two people will always argue what is good and what is bad and so there is a danger that the subject could become too subjective. What is, perhaps, more useful is to ask whether a stand design works. i.e. does it achieve its objectives? If you constantly refer back to what your aims are for the exhibition this will guide the stand design. Let us look at a couple of very different examples:

● First Call Friends Provident is a company offering direct sales in the financial services market. They recently went to the Personal Finance show at Olympia, London. Their prime aim was to take names and addresses for the mailing list of a free booklet which their salespeople could follow up at a

later date.Their main design requirements could be summarised as this: strong corporate identity to underline dealing with a safe secure company, low product identity, high profile for salespeople on the edge of the stand, low requirement for hospitality. The stand was designed along these lines, with six standing-height writing tables positioned around the perimeter. The company took over 1350 names and addresses during the three day show, which the salespeople could then deal with.

● A small pine furniture company took a stand at the Ideal Home Exhibition. Their aim was to sell their products directly from the stand.They had no large sales team to follow up leads and so it was important to do as much business as possible during the show. Their stand was very low on corporate identity, because their name was not important, but their products took a high profile. It was easy for visitors to walk onto the stand and to handle the furniture. Hospitality was good with tea and coffee facilities and all customers were encouraged to stay and spend money. The background stand design was simple so as not to detract from the products.

In both these examples the companies had clearly thought out what they wanted to achieve and how the stand design would have to accommodate their aims. Whatever the size of your stand there are some general rules that you should always consider.

General rules

1. **Sell the company and its products** and not the stand design. It is very easy for all designers to get carried away in their own esoteric fantasy. We often see this in the world of television advertising. Large companies can spend more on a thirty second commercial than you or I could spend in thirty years. They produce adverts that are truly formidable. They intrigue us, they shock us, they make us laugh, they make us wonder. But all too often we forget the particular brand of car / soapsuds / beer that they are advertising. When a visitor walks round an exhibition hall he is not just confronted with four adverts, but more like four hundred. And so it is doubly important that what he remembers is your company and not the amazing designer stand.

At a fundamental level, a good stand design should address the following points:
● What the company wants to achieve.
● Sell the company name.
● Sell the products, services or messages.
● Visitor movements.

Now, depending on what sort of company or organisation you are, you may find that selling your company name, for example, may not be important. Nor may it be relevant that you have many visitors on the stand.But you must consider all four elements above if only to discard one.

2. **Try to be unique**. If your company has strong corporate colours or a particular combination of colours then try to make these prominent on your stand.We can probably all recognise through regular reinforcement the Barclays blue, or the Harrods green. If your company has a particular shape to its logo or its products try to use this in your stand. If your literature is produced in a certain style then try to copy this on your stand.

There is a very harsh test to see if your stand design carries a theme in its own right. Consider the stand without any graphics at all and see if it still conveys what you want it to.

3. Avoid psychological barriers. If you want visitors to walk onto your stand on their own, you should try to make it as easy and as welcoming as possible. We deal with staff attitude in another chapter, but what about "stand attitude"? When you build a stand you are defining a territory, or marking out your patch, which you then want people to enter. Unfortunately it is very easy to put barriers in their way. Visitors have a need to feel comfortable when walking onto a stand; this means that they should not feel they are intruding into a special area nor feel that one foot on the stand and they will be pounced upon by eager sales people.

- The biggest barrier is also the most commonly seen - a step up onto a raised floor. That four inch step probably keeps away more casual visitors than any other device. It is a huge commitment for someone to take that step and it is enough to prevent someone from wandering over to take a look at a display that may have caught his attention. A raised floor is used for three main purposes. Firstly to run electrical cables under the floor to display units. If this can not be avoided by running the cables overhead then try to keep the raised floor back from the edge of the stand. Secondly, it is used to even-up a seriously un-level base floor; there is very little you can do about this other than to lessen the effect of a step by having a ramped section. And thirdly, people specify a raised floor because they have paid a lot of money for that floor space and they are jolly well going to show everyone where the edge of their stand really is.

● Low overhead fascias around the edge of the stand can also be seen as a barrier that discourages people from entering. Again, try to keep these set back.

● Carpet colour. If you really want to avoid delineating the edge of your stand at all, why not use the same carpet colour as in the aisles? One company we have worked with has successfully done this for two years. They have noticed how many people have stopped to look at their displays because it was easy to do so. An unexpected by-product was that the stand also looked much bigger.

● Avoid placing any physical barriers at the edge of the stand e.g. plant troughs or furniture. Only the keenest of the keen will go through an assault course to get on your stand.

4. Use height effectively. Height can be a very powerful tool in making your stand look larger and more impressive. In most major exhibition halls you are allowed to construct up to six meters high. In practice, if you are mainly surrounded by shell scheme stands you need only go up to three meters to look more substantial. In other circumstances a tower of four or five meters will do the trick. The bonus of a high stand is that it can be seen from further away.

5. Consider viewpoints. It is amazing how many stand designers fail to take account of the most simple considerations. The most common mistake, in my view, is to assume that the stand can be best seen and appreciated from a point about five meters opposite. In reality this point is usually to be found in the store room of the stand opposite, or outside the exhibition hall with a brick wall in between. Most exhibition stands are approached from either end, or outside corner first and it is therefore only a small portion of the stand that can be seen from a distance. When a visitor is right up on a stand he is rarely more than one or two meters away because of the confines of the aisle. How should this affect stand design?

● If your stand is in a narrow aisle do not put your company name or main message on a high fascia on the edge of the stand. Visitors will only be able to read it if they contort their necks or use a stepladder brought along specially for the purpose. Better to use the end panels of the walls and to keep any large graphics for the rear of the stand.

● If however your stand can be seen from further away, for example from a central open area, then remember to maximise this opportunity: large signs, height and lights should all be used to their best effect - to promote your stand and company.

● Can your stand be seen from above? Several exhibition halls have a balcony which looks down upon the main hall. At Wembley , for example, the restaurant looks over the entire hall. Most stand designs fail to make use of this huge potential to promote the company name. A simple triangular sign facing upwards can make a big difference to a company's profile and presence at a show.

● Can your stand be seen from below? A balcony position may mean that your stand can be seen from the main body of the hall. However, it is often the back wall of the stand that can be seen and exhibitors do not think of this as having any use. At the recent Restaurant Show at the Business Design Centre Islington only one company on the balcony used its back wall to display its name. Because of this it probably had the highest profile of all exhibitors there.

● Can your stand be seen from the length of a gangway? A position on the edge of the hall may mean that the stand can be seen from a great distance along an aisle. Make the most of it. Put up a big bold tall sign clearly visible above people's heads.

6. Place things of interest near the edge. As we have seen, visitors may be intimidated by the distance to the back of your stand to walk over to see something of interest. This may only be two or three meters, but it is enough to put off some people from making the journey. It is a good idea to try to place your interesting products or displays right on the gangway so that visitors can look, touch and feel the goods before making a commitment. Imagine that you are laying out a shopfront to entice shoppers inside. Now imagine that you put nothing in the shop window at all; you just want people to come into the shop to see what you have to offer. I would suspect that, in the latter case, you would have a very empty shop. But and this is a very big but, do not close off the stand by putting so many things on the edge that visitors can no longer get on.

7. The Three Second Test. It takes someone approximately three seconds to walk past your stand. Can he find out in that time who you are and what you are selling? The prime aim of your stand design is to pass this test. We will discuss this in far more detail in the section "Graphics - do you get the message?" (*page 32*).

8. Stand design and colours. If you do not have dominant corporate colours that you have to use, then you may be fortunate enough to have to choose background colours for the stand. Nearly all shell scheme stands and many larger stands are built in white. This is a safe clean background colour and has the advantage that most graphics and lettering will stand out. Or will they? A white poster on a white wall is really boring. Black letters on a white background are hardly exciting. If you can choose a colour scheme for your stand then you have two immediate advantages:

a) you will look different;

b) you can say something more about your company and its products.

Colours are known to have a whole range of hidden meanings and induce automatic reactions in all of us. Even emotions are often expressed by referring to colours. Car manufacturers were some of the first companies to exploit the colour game. The bottom of the range basic model was offered in light blue, orange or white, all considered to be value for money colours. As you moved up through the range you could get blue or green - good family colours, red - go faster; black - go much faster; metallic silver - executive; gold - seriously expensive. One of the relevant points here is that you could not specify a cheap car in an expensive colour because that would devalue the 'exclusiveness' of the higher priced car.

Our favourite example concerning the importance of colours concerns the sale of mattresses, a product that is completely covered up and hidden for all of its useful life. Now we all know that a cheap mattress is covered with a rough orange and brown floral pattern. And we also know that an expensive mattress is covered with a smooth silver and gold material. Why? Well it is the interior of the mattress that makes the difference and this is invisible. If the manufacturers covered the various quality mattresses all in the same cloth and just priced them differently we would not believe them would we? Because of this conditioning, research has shown that 80% of people cited "colour" as a prime motivator in their choice of mattress. Not bad for a product that is going to be covered up all its life.

So what do colours say about an exhibition stand? Below is a list of colours and the emotions often associated with them.

Here are a few further points to consider when looking at colours.

Try to use light or neutral shades for your walls or backdrop. This will emphasise your graphics rather than compete with them. You can then complement the lighter background with bright coloured beading or decorative trim to pick out any corporate theme.

Never use blue with food products. Blue is the only colour that does not naturally occur in foodstuffs and is only ever associated with mould. The exception to this is the use of blue with chilled or frozen food products. Dark colours tend to enclose

Black:	White:	Red:	Blue:	Green:	Yellow:	Silver and gold:	Orange:
wicked, status disaster, bad luck, good luck, depression, darkness.	clean, goodness, fright, daytime, surrender, modern.	danger, heat, stop, anger, embarrass- ment, war, sin, speed.	calm, sadness, intensity, value for money, male.	nature, environment, fresh, sickness, envy, inexperience.	warmth, summer, cowardice, caution, gold.	experience, age, intelligence, good quality.	warmth, fun, cheapness.

and should be used carefully over large areas.

9. The effective use of lighting Carefully planned lighting can dramatically improve the ambience of a stand. One of the best developments over the last few years has been the better availability of low voltage halogen lighting. This gives off a crisp clear white light which shows up colours to their best. It also gives off less heat which can be a real benefit to staff who are standing all day underneath spotlights. These low voltage systems can also find their way into hitherto inaccessible corners and cabinets, where tiny bulbs can highlight small items. If you want to go down this route it is probably best to talk to a lighting specialist who can advise you on the small details.

Most companies, especially those using shell-scheme stands, entrust their lighting to the appointed electrical contractor. With the best will in the world his interest in the finer points of your stand is minimal. On a good day you could reasonably expect four matching spotlights pointing in roughly the right direction. On a bad day, you might get an old fluorescent tube hanging on two bits of string. If lighting is important you should specify as many details as you can. Here are a few points to watch out for:

● Ask about the general conditions in the exhibition hall. The Barbican in London, for example, has low ceilings and can heat up very quickly indeed. The Grand Hall at Olympia has far more natural light and is generally less stuffy.

● Heat can build up quickly in enclosed areas and especially under false ceilings, even thin muslin.

● Harsh spotlights may show up minute flaws in some polished surfaces. It may be better to use diffused lights in these circumstances.

● For advanced lighting buffs, there are some superb singing and dancing spotlights available. These can shine your company logo onto a wall, move it round, change its colour etc. Ask specialists for advice.

10. Plants The stand-designing cynic says that you should only use plants on your stand when you have run out of other ideas. While no-one wants their stand to look like a greenhouse, this attitude is perhaps a little unfair. An exhibition environment can be very harsh, with lots of strong bright colours and it can be very advantageous to soften things down a little with some greenery. A few well-positioned plants can enhance the overall ambience of your stand, especially in hospitality areas.

11. What products to show As a general observation, companies tend to show too much on their stand. Remember that in the first instance you only have about three seconds to show a visitor an overall picture of what you are selling. If you put too much on your stand this message may become too confused. On the other hand you will want to show a broad range of products to the thirty three per cent of visitors who are new to the industry and may want some in-depth information about your company.

● If you sell products, make your major display

about something that is new, or innovative or inherently interesting. You can then show your other products in a less prominent display, or even show them with photographs and brochures. Show machines that are working or products that are in use; movement and activity always attracts interest.

● If you are selling a service, try to make a display of the benefits of that service. Try to avoid the old clichés of 'save time - save money' because these have become so over-used as to be meaningless.

● If you are selling something intangible such as a message, for example road safety or health education, then a display of some items associated with that message may be interesting. You could show for example a shattered windscreen, or how a driver's airbag works, or the inevitable results of smoking.

12. Do you need a hospitality area? A couple of years ago I was dealing with a company who were talking about their design brief for their exhibition stand which was to be about 100m^2. Their priorities ran something like this: first we want a large kitchen and rest room for our staff. It should have comfortable seating for eight, kitchen sink, fridge, tea and coffee etc. After that we need a large meeting room for important clients, with meeting table and six upright chairs. And then just design the stand around it. As it turned out the stand was built along those lines and guess what happened? The staff spent all their time recuperating and drinking coffee, the meeting room was never used and the rest of the stand no-one cared about.

So when should you have a hospitality area? Perhaps we should turn the question round and ask: "Do your visitors wish to be entertained?" There are some companies whose main purpose for going to an exhibition is to entertain existing clients. They issue smart invitations, provide good food and drink and have an enclosed hospitality suite on their stand. If your business depends to a great extent on personal contacts, then this welcoming approach is probably a good idea. It has the added bonus that while you are holding your client on your stand he can not go visiting the competitors. I must, however, raise two small objections. Firstly is this the best way to entertain your existing customers? Could it not be done more effectively and more personally during the normal course of business? Secondly, while looking after existing customers, is there not a danger that you may be ignoring new ones, or even alienating those who did not get an invitation? For this reason you should be very careful that a hospitality area does not take over the stand.

Of course, for most medium-size stands, a hospitality area just means a few comfortable chairs around a coffee table. There is nothing wrong with this except that your own staff must not use it as their rest area. Unfortunately, furniture hire from the official contractors is quite expensive. But do not be tempted to bring your own cheap folding chairs from the local discount store. Or even worse, inexpensive white garden furniture. This will always look cheap and nasty and will reflect badly on your company. It would even be better to strip out your office for a few days and bring the furniture to the exhibition hall.

Further ideas
Can your stand design tie-in with your current advertising campaign?

It may be possible to take the best elements from an advertising campaign and to reproduce them on your stand. The best example I ever saw of this was by the snack food company Phileas Fogg. Their well known television adverts featured a globe of the world with a large arrow pointing to the company factory at Medomsley Road, Conset. At the IFE Exhibition at Earls Court their stand was dominated by a huge globe, about five meters tall, with the same arrow pinpointing that infamous town in Co. Durham. This provided a simple but effective link between a high profile advertising campaign and a trade exhibition. From the visitor's point of view it meant that there was fast recognition of the stand and its products.

Does your stand have to look like an exhibition stand at all? In our travels we've seen a giant pin-ball machine, a ten meter high waterfall and a junkyard.

Briefing a stand designer/contractor
If you are organising a stand for the first time you should always consider inviting two or three contractors to tender for the job. Competition is fierce and so it is easy to get different ideas and different prices from various contractors. The quality of their own presentation may well be an indicator as to the quality of their stand design and build skills.

Stand designers and contractors should always tender at first on a speculative basis. This means that their initial designs and proposal are free. It is unreasonable therefore to expect too much detail at this stage but you should get some good overall design proposals with ideas for graphics and finishes.

Before you brief a stand designer you should already have some basic information to hand. This should obviously include the name, place, time and date of the show, contact numbers for the organisers, size and position of the stand. After that, you should aim to give the designer as much information as possible to help him translate your ideas into something tangible. Here are a few guidelines.

1. In the first instance you should stress to a designer your aims and objectives for going to a show. Explain that no matter how good the stand looks, its main purpose is to help achieve those aims and objectives.

2. Describe the products, services or messages to be sold. Do they have any special requirements e.g. heavy duty power, air, gas or water supply? Are there any industry standards in displaying these products?

3. How many people will be working on the stand? How many people do you hope to have visiting the stand?

4. What are your minimum requirements for stor-

age or office space?

5. Do you need literature displays?

6. What are your views on hospitality? How would you prefer to entertain people on your stand?

7. Are there any corporate colour schemes or product colour schemes that need priority?

8. Budget - discuss how much money you have to spend on the design and build element of your exhibition. Remember that this is only one part of your overall budget. It is necessary to tell a designer how much you have to spend in order that he does not waste his time on a project that you cannot afford.

9. Stand dressing. You should make it clear at the outset how far you expect the stand contractors to go. Many misunderstandings arise when installing equipment, or doing the final dressing of the stand. If these are discussed well in advance then there should be no problems.

10. Ownership and multi-use stands. One of the big grey areas of stand building is who owns what and it is well worth talking this through with a potential contractor. If he is building a one-off stand it is normal that he does so on a "hire only" basis which means that after the show he will dump it or break it up for other things. If you want to use the same stand for several shows throughout the year, it is very important to discuss this at the briefing stage. It will affect the way the stand is built and dismantled and the contractor may wish to discuss storage charges. If you only want to do one show per year then you should discuss with a contractor what he

will do with the walls and other elements, whether he will have them available for the following year and whether the graphics will be re-usable.

What happens next

Your stand contractor should come back to you in an agreed time with one or more proposals. Where possible, ask him to produce a small model of his design because this is much easier to envisage than drawings. The main problem with perspective drawings and artist's impressions is that they give false ideas about size. A drawing can make a stand look large, interesting and sophisticated whereas in reality it is small, boxy and plain. Equally, I am no great fan of computer graphics with a 'walk-through' facility. It is all too easy to be impressed by the advanced computer wizardry and ignore the small details of the stand design itself. Call me old fashioned but I think there is no substitute for showing a 3-D product with a 3-D model of it.

When looking at comparative quotations, check very carefully what is included. The main items which are often missed are:
● Electrical supply and connections
● Graphics
● Furniture hire
● Stand storage

Once you have chosen a design that best suits your aims then you should firm up some of the smaller details with the contractor and let him get on with it.

Summary

● Sell the company and it's products or services not the stand design.
● Try to be unique.
● Avoid barriers which stop the visitors walking on to your stand.
● Use height effectively.
● Consider from what position the visitor will see your stand.
● Position your most interesting displays near the edge.
● Can the visitor understand your message in the 3 seconds it takes to walk past your stand.
● Good lighting can make a considerable difference to your stand.
● Use plants and foliage to soften your overall image and not to make your stand look like a garden centre.
● Put as few products on display as possible.
● Do you need a hospitality area?
● When briefing your stand designer/constructor, give them as musch information as possible to enable them to achieve your objectives.

In this section we consider the importance of graphics - all the signs, letters, words, names and posters that we put all over an exhibition stand.

Good graphics can make or break an exhibition stand. Let me explain why they are so important. An exhibition stand on its own is merely a structure for conveying a message. To draw an analogy, it is the billboard without the poster. Now, we have seen that there are many things you can do to make sure that the billboard does its job better; you can put it in the right place, make sure it is the right size, shape, colour and make sure it is well lit. It can be enhanced in many ways, but until it has its message stuck on it is never more than a blank billboard.

The Three Second Test

A visitor takes about three seconds to walk past your stand and in those three seconds he will read the first big messages to catch his attention. It is these messages that will influence his decision to stop, maybe stop, or to walk on.

In this respect, an exhibition stand is very similar to certain forms of advertising. When you flick through a magazine, you will probably stop to read just a few of the full page adverts. But which ones? It is thought that an advert has less than three seconds to catch your attention. If you are intrigued by the headline, or if you are interested by some other part

of the message you will then read more. But if the headline does not interest you or hold any further promise then you will probably turn the page.

And so it is with exhibition stands. You must grab the attention of a visitor within a very short space of time or he will walk on by. In addition, you should then provide some further information to back up the headline.

Good graphics must work on three levels:

1. The three second message. This is the hook or the draw to get someone interested in your products. It often contains a promise e.g. "More Comfortable Furniture."

2. The ten second message. The secondary stage to give a little more information about the first message and to fulfil the promise e.g. "New design padding means that our chairs fit your body better".

3. Further information. This need not be a poster on the wall but could be a leaflet or brochure or even the products themselves e.g. more information about the design, construction and features of the furniture.

We need to take a good look at all of these to see why many companies get them wrong.

Quantity

The biggest and the most common mistake for exhibitors is to put too many graphics on their stand. It is quite normal to see large posters with hundreds of words of text extolling the virtues of a product. The truth is that they will never be read. Even posters with seven or eight 'bullet' points showing the main benefits of a product are often too long. If you put several posters like this around your stand then the chances are that the whole message will become lost or confused. Why?

Imagine you are going down into an underground station to catch a train. Advertising posters there take three distinct forms. Firstly there are the adverts you see on the side of the escalators. These are always extremely brief - company name - product name - benefit. Probably no more than five words maximum. There is simply no point in putting anything more there because people can not stop and read. Secondly there are posters in the walkways or tunnels leading to the platforms. Here you will see poster sites with slightly more information; perhaps a contact number or an address, ticket prices for a show, or an advert for a local business. People walking past will still have a short attention span but at least they do have the chance to stop. Thirdly, there are the poster sites on the platform or on the wall opposite. Have you ever noticed how these are usually packed full of information or include long stories, or even have long company histories to enhance their product?. The reason is obvious. You will always have a few minutes waiting for the train when you have the time and the willingness to devour long messages.

So, where is your exhibition stand in the underground station of advertising? To an extent it will depend on what sort of company you are, but your graphics should either be the 'escalator' type or the 'walkway' type. You should never plan to have graphics of the 'platform' type because they will never be read; no-one has the time or willingness to stand and read long copy. There is, perhaps, only one exception to this: if you have a stand next to a snack bar where there are queues then people may have time to read more than twenty words.

Company name

Do you spend thousands of pounds every year to promote your company name? Do people see your company name and immediately associate it with your products, your quality service, your style? Take a look at this list:

Mars	Black & Decker	Microsoft
J.C.B.	Vauxhall	Heinz
Sainsbury's	Gillette	Bosch
Hoover	Butler and Co.	Hogg Engineering
James Rackley	Premier Services	Conquest Ltd.
	F.L.G. Computers.	

How does your company name compare to these? Are you one of the former or one of the latter? In most industries, the companies who are well known are the ones who carry out a lot of corporate identity advertising. This is to enhance the feel-good factor when you buy their products. It is these companies who can safely put their name on their exhibition stand with little further explanation. But if you are a less well known company, then you should be extremely careful about how you use your company name. For example, at a recent public exhibition there were two large stands selling sundry kitchen items under the huge company name of:

GEORGE F. WOODSIDE LTD.

This name went right across the stands and completely dominated any other signs. Now, I do not know Mr. Woodside and I have never heard of his company and I am sure he is a very nice man. But I am also sure he has an ego the size of a jumbo-jet because his name was totally irrelevant to the stand, to the products and to what he was trying to achieve. How much better it would have been if the main sign above the stand was:

AMAZING KITCHEN GADGETS!

Setting up an exhibition stand is very different to setting up a high street shop where you need to encourage people to use you over a long period of time. At an exhibition you have one chance in one day to show someone what you have to offer. The problem with most corporate names is they do not give any clue as to what the company actually does. For every Kwik-Fit Tyres there are at least two John Smith Enterprises. Unfortunately, at exhibitions, the vast majority of shell scheme stands seem to be taken by John Smiths. "But," they say, "we want peo-ple to remember our name!". This is misguided. What you want is people to remember your product. It is far better to use valuable graphic space to describe your product and its benefits than to show the name of the trading company. If I had to invent a rule for this it would be: product benefits before name unless you already spend thousands of pounds on promotions in the corporate identity game. It's not very snappy but if you say it often enough you can just about get the 'name' and 'game' to rhyme.

Product features and benefits

It is quite common to see a product on display, or a photo of a product, with a long list of 'bullet points' or features.It is far less common to see a simple statement of benefit, despite the fact that all sales research shows that people buy on benefits not features. Here is a quick re-cap on features and benefits:

Features - describe the physical characteristics of a product. For example if you were describing a pen you could say: it has a retractable nib, a metal case and a ribbed end.

Benefits - describe the advantages of those features to a user. For example you would say about the pen: it does not stain your pocket, it is difficult to break and your fingers do not slip off the end when writing.

The simple theory is that no matter how many amazing features a product has we will not buy it until we see the benefits.

At an exhibition the purpose of the main graphics are to catch the visitor's attention. He would be far more impressed by a simple statement of benefits and to leave a long list of features to the 'further information' section. If you get really stuck trying to think of the benefits of your products, do not forget that the price may be the main benefit. If so do not be afraid to show it.

Lets look at a few examples.

● We have seen that George F. Woodside could have called his stand 'Amazing Kitchen Gadgets.' But this still does not convey any real benefits. How about:

TIME-SAVING KITCHEN GADGETS
or KITCHEN GADGETS THAT SAVE YOU TIME AND MONEY

Or why not put a big promise in there too:

KITCHEN GADGETS GUARANTEED TO SAVE YOU TIME AND MONEY

Some purists might say that this is a pretty strange name for an exhibition stand, but I say "why?" It conveys everything a potential visitor to your stand needs to know and arouses his curiosity.

● Once a year at Birmingham there is the Industrial Controls and Instrumentation Show. This may sound like the 'exhibition from hell' to you but I am assured that it is absolutely fascinating to those in the industry. Several companies sell Depth Gauges and Flow Meters. These are usually marked with large graphics that say:

DEPTH GAUGES AND FLOW METERS

Now this is not very enterprising or interesting.

How about adding a benefit:

EASILY INSTALLED DEPTH GAUGES
or GUARANTEED ACCURATE FLOW METERS

And how about using one of the finest tricks in the advertisers book by turning a statement into a question:

HOW OUR DEPTH GAUGES ARE EASILY INSTALLED and WHY OUR FLOW METERS ARE GUARANTEED ACCURATE

Both these headlines now invite further investigation. Even I may be tempted to go onto the stand.

● And now an example of a company that got it right. The Housewares International Show is a trade exhibition where manufacturers and wholesalers sell to retailers. A manufacturer of triangular garden clothes-lines had a stand where the main graphic was:

FASTER DRYING CLOTHES

The company name and the product name were on the stand but much less prominent and only of secondary importance. I can even remember why these clothes lines worked faster: -

More space between lines,
Higher frames
Easier swivel action.

The important thing to note here is that the benefit of the product is the main headline graphic. Features come afterwards. Just imagine what this company could have put on a poster; 'Slough Tubular Enterprises (Manufacturing) Ltd., are pleased to display their improved GCD3 model rotary action clothes drier which features a new PTFE bearing and longer central shaft...'

Some of the fastest growing exhibitions recently have been in the food industry. There are many small manufacturers who put their name on the stand and then show off all their products on display shelves. Some even offer tastings. Now it is very difficult with food to talk about features and benefits without resorting to old cliches like: tasty, ready prepared, top quality, easy to cook etc. Try to think of additional benefits that really make the difference. In the catering sector this usually does not refer to the food at all but to its distribution. So instead of a sign that says;

PENNINE VALLEY FOODS
Fine foods from Cumbria
How about
PENNINE VALLEY FOODS
Next-day delivery to your door

Other benefits for food products may also include portion control, packaging or nationwide service. The main thing to remember when thinking about your stand graphics is to find something that is a real benefit to your potential customers.

Pictures

It is true that pictures tell a thousand words. And good exhibition pictures can tell even more. Modern production techniques allow you to produce enormous full colour photos that can make a real impact on your stand. Many of the latest "pop-up" stands

use a photo to cover the entire back wall and this has two great advantages. Firstly , you can illustrate a product which is too big to bring onto your stand. Secondly, if you do not sell a product but a service or a message then a photo can give an overall idea of what you do. A few examples:

● If you are selling your hotel conference facilities then a large photo of the meeting rooms is a lot easier than trying to describe them. All you need to add then is a few words to show the benefits e.g. 'two minutes from Heathrow, or 'with bedrooms for five hundred'.

● If you are selling membership of a club or organisation then a few good photos of the club's activities can save a lot of explaining.

● If you are selling a message such as road safety then there is no end to the type of photos you could use to attract attention.

● If you are an architect or civil engineer then some impressive photos of your best projects will be much better than displaying your drawing board.

● Some computer companies have finally worked out that if the object of their product is to save time , then the benefit to the user is that he should have more leisure time. These companies have now taken to selling their product by showing a large photo of a man playing golf, or a couple lying on the beach. Nice try, computer companies! But we all know that it just does not work like that.

● Beware of showing photos of the same subject that all your competitors show. At a recent show concerned with telecommunications and voice transmission, (Voice '93 at Olympia) most stands had pictures of happy smiley people talking into telephones. We persuaded our client to put up large photos of an extremely angry man shouting into his 'phone. It was a fine example of the dangers of not using this company's voice mail software.

If you are looking for unusual photos then try phoning around the larger photo libraries (look in yellow pages) as they have thousands of standard shots that can be used for exhibitions. Their fees for one-off use at an exhibition are quite reasonable.

Diagrams

Complex technical diagrams fall into the same category as posters with too much text. No-one ever studies them and they usually waste space. Steer clear of them in the same way as you would traffic bollards.

Words and phrases

There are certain buzz-words that you should always try to include in your graphics. These should come as no surprise:

NEW   FREE   SEX   IMPROVED   GREEN

I am sure that if you could think of a product where you could use all of these you could have an instant advertising success. The word 'green' is fashionable because of its association with environmental issues and still generates added interest in nearly all products.

Things to avoid

● The word 'quality' has become so over used that it is now meaningless. If you find yourself about to use it, ask yourself what you are really trying to say. For example, you sell 'Quality Furniture'. Do you mean cheap-end-of-the-market-but-good-value-for-money? Or do you mean hand-made-heavy-duty-hard-wearing-high-specification? Try to find any other phrase that best sums up the essence of your product or service.

● Puns and wordplay. Open any local newspaper and you will find the worst type of home-made advertising anywhere: 'Don't be a Drip, Roof Repairs by John.' 'Hair Care with Flair at Snippers' 'Go Bananas at Harry's Fruit Shop!' I do not think that people roll around the floor laughing at this sort of thing any more than I believe that I would rush out to that establishment to part with good money. Don't even think of trying this. It is true, however, that most large advertising agencies use puns and wordplay as their stock in trade. Look at roadside billboards and you will see some fine examples. Here are two that left a lasting impression on me:

CALLING TOOTING AND BARKING (ad. for B.T.)
NINETY HORSES, ONE CAT, NO BULL (ad. for a Ford car)

The reason these work is that they are unusual and unexpected and some very clever people were paid lots of money to think them up. It is most probable that fifty percent of the population do not understand the advert or what they are trying to advertise but that is another matter.

● Humour. Some people have very strange ideas about humour and work not mixing. These people are more than likely to be your boss. As with puns, avoid unless you really know what you are doing.

● Clichés. These are any words or phrases that have become tired and worn out:

"We are pleased to promote our latest ..."

"Announcing our new model ZX5 ..."

"Tomorrow's products today ..."

"Leading-edge technology ..."

"Solutions to every problem ..."

"A New Era is dawning in ..."

It is extremely difficult to think of new catch-phrases, slogans, straplines or endorsements, but try you must.

Some technical stuff about graphics

Graphic production has become a highly specialised field recently. Hand painted signs and hand-cut lettering are very rare. Computer guided cutters will make letters, logos and diagrams in almost any material. There is an enormous choice of typefaces and styles. All this means that you are best advised to entrust this work to someone who knows what they are doing. The business pages of your local telephone book will yield an array of signwriters. In my experience there are a couple of very important factors to consider when choosing a signwriter.

● Choose someone local. You will save a vast amount of time and money when it comes to view-ing and approving.

● Choose someone who has a compatible computer system to your own; it is then very easy to transfer copy, designs, logo etc.

● Choose someone who has a fax machine.

● Choose someone who appears to know the meaning of the word 'deadline'

● Choose someone who can spel.

When talking to a signwriter or graphic designer, it is helpful to know a little about some of the options and the technical background to what is available.

Pre-spaced vinyl lettering

This is now the most common way of producing text for signs of all sizes. A computer guided machine cuts out the letters from sticky back plastic and they are all loaded onto a backing sheet, perfectly spaced and ready to be applied to almost any surface. There is a wide choice of fonts, styles, colours, textures and sizes. Complex logos can be reproduced by scanning them into the computer. This is the best method for producing one-off signs, but if you need a larger quantity of the same sign (say fifteen or more copies) then a form of printing will be more suitable.

Cut-out lettering

Computer guided machines will also cut out letters from thicker materials such as polystyrene, cork and plastic. These will then stand out from the surface they are mounted on. These letters can be faced or painted in most colours, or they can look very effective if covered in metallic gold or silver. If cut out of clear plastic they can be backlit.

Screen printing

This is a method for printing on to flat surfaces where vinyl lettering may not be suitable. It is possible to screen print onto almost any surface including cloth, plastic, painted finishes and it is also possible to print onto manufactured items such as wooden panels or plastic folders. It can be expensive if you are not doing large quantities as most of the money is spent on set-up costs.

Litho printing

This is what you would call 'normal' printing onto paper or card. It is only feasible to use printing if you are producing large quantities of posters or signs as, once again, most of the costs are in setting up.

Photocopying

If you can produce a good black and white original then there is no reason why you should not have this blown up on a good photocopier. Some graphics bureaux can now blow up to A1 size from an A4 original. If you get this mounted and laminated it can look as smart as anything else.

Laser colour copying

This, also, can be a very cost effective way to produce small colour posters. Modern machines have good resolution, but much will depend on the quality of the original.

Black and white photos

One of the easiest ways to produce a poster containing a quantity of text is to produce an original and to have it blown up photographically. You will need to get an original with a finer print quality than the average office printer. If you produce the original on computer, then take the disk to a specialised bureau that can output it at 'bromide' quality; about 2000 dots per inch. When this is blown up you will get much crisper lines and text.

Colour photos

When enlarging a colour photo to poster size you really do need to start from an original with good colour and sharp focus. If finances permit, always use a professional photographer, or consider buying in a photo from a photo library.

Mounting and sealing

One of the nastiest things to see at an exhibition is a well-produced poster or photo just stuck to the wall using sticky tape. All posters should be mounted onto a background board to make them rigid. Mounting boards are usually made from 'Foamex' or 'Foamboard' and it is worth noting the difference. Foamex is a heavier, solid, expanded plastic sheet that is difficult to dent or break. Foamboard (sometimes called foamcore) is very lightweight and is made from a polystyrene core sandwiched between two sheets of card. It is fairly rigid but does tend to bow when in large format and a photo is mounted on one side. It is also very easy to damage the corners or edges if you drop it.

If your photo is likely to be in an area where it will be touched or brushed it is worth getting it 'sealed' or 'laminated'. This is a protective plastic covering that gives your photo a hardwearing washable finish.

Back-lit photos
Some graphics can be considerably enhanced if they are mounted on a back-lit light box. This is the sort of thing that you often see on shopfronts where the lettering or photo is illuminated from behind. This work should always be entrusted to specialists.

Type terminology
A few words that you may not be familiar with:
Ascender: The part of lower-case letters which extends upwards e.g. on b d h k
Baseline: The line on which characters sit.
Descender: The part of lower case letters that extends downwards e.g. on j p q y
Font: A particular design of letters, also known as a (type)face. Many people use the term 'font' and 'typeface' interchangeably.
Kerning: Adjusting the space between letters, i.e. moving them closer or further apart.

Lower Case: Letters that are not capitals; e.g. a b c d e f
Point / Point Size: A point is the unit of measure used in sizing typefaces. There are roughly 72 points to the inch. The point size of a font is measured from the top of the tallest ascender to the bottom of the lowest descender.
Serif: The 'foot' or cross-piece at the end of the main strokes of a letter. A typeface is usually either a serif or a sanserif face. Two of the best known typefaces are Times (serif) and Helvetica (sanserif).
Upper-case: Letters that are capitals; e.g. A B C D E F
The importance of good graphic presentation on your stand cannot be over-estimated. Whether you are arranging graphics yourself, or you are asking your stand contractor to organise things, it will help if you put in some serious time and effort to think about what you want to achieve. Armed with a little information you should be able to make your stand the one that attracts attention.

Summary
- Be big, bold, and simple. You have less than three seconds to get your message across.
- Keep it brief. No-one reads long panels of text.
- Sell your product, not the company name.
- Stress the benefits, not the features.
- Use appropriate photos.
- Use the sales buzzwords.
- Avoid clichés.

In this section we look at the games, gimmicks and activities that people arrange on their stands in order to attract attention. Research shows that the average visitor spends five hours at a show and stops at twelve stands, half of which were pre-planned. What is it then that attracts a visitor onto six other stands? It could be a good product display, it could be good graphics and it could be enticing activities. Of course, if you can organise all three then visitors should be queuing up. If you organise none, then someone may just walk onto your stand and say "hello, tell me about your company and your products, I am very interested and I have a bottomless bank account." This may seem unlikely to you, but it is clear that 50% of exhibitors believe it will happen because their stands are about as interesting as an empty bus shelter.

But there is one golden rule that must be considered: stand activities must be used as a means to an end, not as an end in themselves. By this, I mean that once you have created some interest you should capitalise on it by moving onto another stage in the sales process: the object is to talk to people and find out if they have an interest in your products.

Building an 'edge'

Let's use the analogy of a busy market place in a town centre with lots of traders all vying for your attention. They have their products out on display and hundreds of people are walking past. Sounds familiar? A few of the smarter traders do what they call building an edge. This is giving themselves an advantage over their competitors by doing anything from shouting loudly to waving their products around or putting on a special display. A chap I remember sold vast amounts of crockery by piling up and balancing an entire dinner service on one arm which he would then offer for less than a few pounds. Of course he would drop the lot with a tremendous noise, but by then he had his audience.

Another trick of market traders is to use cheap giveaways to attract attention. One television sold for only five pounds to the lady at the back. A complete stereo system for two pounds. A set of bathroom towels for 50 pence. Once again the object is to attract a crowd so that the real selling can start. And of course a crowd of people will always attract more people who want to see what is going on.

The lesson to be learned is simple: use gimmicks as a way of getting attention but you must have a secondary purpose and a way of dealing with it.

Demonstrations

The easiest and arguably the most effective form of stand activity is to put on a working display of your own products or services. This is immediately relevant and should enhance the overall message of your stand. When I suggest this, many people have complained to me that their products are not suitable for a practical demonstration. The most common one is that they sell capital equipment which cannot be used for an interesting working demonstration; a fridge, a desk, computer hardware, guttering, books. The golden rule here is not to show your product on its own, but show what it does. Here are a few examples of how some companies have successfully conquered this problem.

● Shell Gas sell a product that is either invisible, or contained in an ugly cylinder. Difficult to show - eh? On their stand they featured a skilled glass-blower who used bottled gas for his blowtorch. During the show he attracted a constant crowd while he made wonderful coloured glass ornaments.

● Redland Roof tiles had a craftsman making special ornamental tiles from clay. They also built a small belfry style roof space where they had a display by the Bat Preservation Society of Great Britain.

● At the Food Ingredients Exhibition a chocolate manufacturer set up a complete hot chocolate vat with a chocolate fountain which then fed into a machine that could produce novelty shapes. Not surprisingly this was a very popular stand.

● At the Materials Handling Exhibition there was a manufacturer of hooks. Just plain boring metal hooks. The only interesting thing about hooks is what you can hang from them. This company suspended a Ferrari, upright, two feet above the ground. That seemed to do the trick.

So what can you do if you sell fridges? How about giving away chilled orange juice on the stand? Or, try packing the fridge with eggs and asking people to guess the number. If you sell plastic guttering think about creating a complex waterfall feature using the product to channel streams of water. If you sell office furniture, create a destructive display to show how robust it is.

Games

Most companies try organising some sort of game on their stand at some time in their exhibition cycle. The object of these games is often not clearly thought out, but seems to be to collect business cards from visitors. The games themselves can be quite popular. I have regularly seen a golf putting game and a basketball game with automatic scoring. The problem with these two is they bear no relevance to the products being sold. There is a major problem here: I spend five minutes shooting a ball into a net and then the salesman asks me "what is your interest in plastic moulding machinery?" None at all and he has just wasted five minutes. After a few visitors like me the salesman will probably stop asking the question altogether and just concentrate on playing the game.

Other games are actually designed to collect business cards. Exchange your business card for three ping pong balls and throw one into a glass jar to win a prize. I once saw an ingenuous carousel affair where you had to insert your business card into a turntable at exactly the right moment to dislodge a key that would open a prize box. With these sort of games it is very rare to go on to discuss the products that the company is actually selling. The exhibiting company ends up with a pile of business cards which are unqualified leads. When a salesman comes to follow up these leads he will be rejected nine times out of ten and will probably give up after twenty. If you want a list of people who attended the exhibition buy it from the organisers, it will be cheaper.

Giveaways and promotional items

In contrast, giveaways on your stand have a very different purpose. Giveaways should be a corporate PR exercise, whereby visitors take away a small item with your company name and phone number that they will hopefully look at for a long time. The most popular items are, of course, pens and key - rings. But if you open any incentives magazine you will see hundreds of ideas for little freebies. These include hats, diaries, toys, cheque book holders, paper clips, tea-towels, pen-knives, paper pads etc.

The most important thing to remember about giveaways is that you have to actually give them away. There is absolutely no point in taking half of them back to the office with you to sit in a cupboard for years. The tendency is to give gifts to existing customers or to people who you think are good potential business. The truth is that once you have paid for two or three thousand gifts, they cost the same if you give away only ten or if you give away all three thousand. If giveaways are to be effective as a PR tool then they should have at least your company name, what you do and a contact number.

Plastic carrier bags appear by the zillion at most trade shows. The idea is that visitors will carry your name around the exhibition hall and also take it home with them. Carrier bags get filled with all the exhibition brochures and leaflets that are taken and never read. As each new company gives a visitor a carrier bag with leaflets he stuffs it inside the first one he got. There are therefore only two effective ways of giving out carrier bags: either get pole position right next to the entrance so that yours is the first and 'outer' carrier bag, or make your bag so large and so rigid that it can not be folded inside someone else's.

Free prize draws

At many smaller shows there are enough free Champagne draws to launch a fleet for the Swiss Navy. These are not only old hat, but they are also no longer attractive. And at best, all you end up with is a pile of unqualified leads. A prize draw should only be used if your staff are trained to use it as an approach to a visitor who they will then qualify. Otherwise think of something more exciting.

Special features

Some exhibitors successfully use a special feature to attract interest. This could be anything from a waterfall to a giant working model or an inflatable monster. Handled correctly, these can be a great crowd puller. A company selling a water treatment system at the Ideal Home Exhibition had a maze of enormous plumbing pipes over the stand leading into a tropical fish tank. The whole stand looked attractive and fun. Visitors stopped to look at the fish where they were easy prey for the salespeople.

Hospitality people

A few years ago, almost every major show would come complete with dozens of attractive models draped over every car, truck or boat, especially on press days, dragging in the media and subsequently the crowds. Times have changed. Now it has become politically incorrect to use sex to promote products. After all, it might alienate half of your potential audience. It is now very rare to see 'hospitality people' staffing a stand. That is not to say that you should not employ temporary staff at all; but visitors do prefer to deal with knowledgeable, regular sales staff . Temporary exhibition staff are available from several agencies and with proper briefing, they can be excellent for prospecting and identifying your potential customers.

Pre-planned competitions

If you can target your audience before a show then the 'carry card' technique can be very successful. This is sometimes known as a 'delayed fulfilment' competition or gift. This involves sending out a card or gift prior to the show which is somehow incomplete, or the solution is only available on the stand. Visitors wishing to know if they have won must then come onto your stand to find out, which gives an opportunity to open a sales conversation. Here are a few tried and tested examples.

● Send out a large jigsaw piece which will win a prize if it fits the gap in the puzzle on the stand.

● Send out a card containing brainteasers or puzzles with the solutions only available on the stand.

● Send out a prize cheque for £1000 which is valid only if its number matches one on the stand.

● Send out a card printed with 'secret ink' that can only be developed by a complicated process only known to the stand staff (usually UV light).

● Send a card where the prize is printed in a barcode, where the decoder is on the stand.

If you target your audience well you can get a stunning response rate from this sort of activity.

Summary

If you want stand activities to work they must be:

● Fun

● Relevant.

● Easy to use and participate.

● Low key enough not to take over the stand.

● Popular with stand staff (or they will ensure that they do not work!)

This section of the book deals with the many opportunities to communicate your message and get effective public relations from your exhibitions. Exhibitions are normally the focus of activity for an industry sector and as they are normally sponsored by the leading magazine there are many opportunities for getting very wide coverage of your message. The message you wish to get across falls into three parts - before the show, during the show and after the show.

Some exhibitors believe that once they have booked the space the responsibility for getting the visitors to the exhibition is that of the organisers. To a certain extent this is true. When you are booking the space you will have found out from the organisers how many visitors they are expecting and the more professional ones will be able to tell you what their marketing plan is for increasing this number. For large public exhibitions then the organisers may even be advertising the exhibition on the television or on radio. In fact some of the fastest growing public exhibitions are spin off's from television programmes. So why do you need to advertise your presence at the exhibition?

Attracting the visitor

Visitors at exhibitions attend with a "shopping list" of exhibitors that they are going to see. This list is very important as a visitor will only stop at and have a meaningful conversation at between ten and fifteen stands. It is therefore imperative that you get on to as many visitors' shopping lists as possible.

How to get on to the visitors' shopping list.
Here are a few suggestions that have worked for us:
● Invitations
Most organisers will either send you or when asked will provide you with complementary tickets to the exhibition. In some cases they will also overprint these tickets with your company name and the stand number. You should send out these tickets to as many of your existing customers and potential customers as possible. Better still you should send your favoured customers a personal letter and the invitation. Most companies have a list of people who have either stopped trading with them or who have yet to be turned into customers. Now is the time to find that list and invite those people to your stand.

Carry cards
This is an American expression for a leaflet sent to customers which invites them to bring it to the stand in order to win a prize or to get some form of special treatment.

One company that was a wholesaler decided to send out different types of carry cards to their customers. They had exactly the same message printed on all three cards and the only difference was that they printed one in blue (the company house colour), one in silver and one in gold. They distributed the blue ones through the leading trade magazine. They sent a copy of the silver one to every one of their account customers and they sent the gold one to the customers who had purchased a new product during the last twelve months. The result was that the customers who received all three knew that they were important and in some cases turned up on the stand with all three cards. The stand staff were able to quickly identify the really good prospects, i.e. the gold card holders who were known to be buyers of new products. Equally anyone with a silver card was an existing customer and those with a blue card were potential customers.

There are many ways of producing interesting carry cards including:

● Bring this to our stand for a free cup of coffee
● The free prize draw. Bring this card to win a trip to America
● The competition card

Carry cards do not necessarily have to be posted in advance of the exhibition. They can, with the organisers permission be handed out at the entrance to the hall. I have even seen them handed out at London's Euston station to everyone travelling to the exhibition in Birmingham. You can also hire the headrests of the courtesy coaches that bring the customers from the car park to the exhibition hall and put your carry cards in them.

Some exhibitors go even further and send out keys which will open a safe or jigsaw pieces that fit into a special promotion panel on the stand. See the chapter on stand activities (*page 41*) for more information.

Advertising

There are many opportunities for advertising around an exhibition. You can advertise in the exhibition previews, the catalogue itself, or indeed, in the follow-up articles in magazines after the exhibition. Remember than your main aim is to get visitors on to your stand and therefore your advert should give them some reason for visiting the stand.

Many exhibition catalogues are used by the visitor as a reference manual for the rest of the year so the catalogue can be a very effective form of advertising. If one of your exhibition aims is to upset your competitors then it can be worthwhile advertising on the back of the catalogue so that your competitors are faced with your company name every time a visitor walks onto their stand holding the catalogue. Some visitors get the catalogue on entering the exhibition and then they find somewhere to sit down and go through it marking off the stands that they want to visit.

There are also endless opportunities to advertise at the venue and in some cases on the way to the venue. You can hire sandwich boards, full poster sites around the exhibition hall and advertise your message on them. There may also be opportunities to advertise in the hall itself.

I know from my own experience that when faced with yet another call from the organisers trying to sell me advertising space I am tempted to say "no" out of hand. After all this exhibition business is very expensive. However, a well thought out advert can bring many new valuable visitors to the stand.

If you do advertise then ask the magazine how much free editorial space you are going to get. I know that editors space can not be bought with advertising but just occasionally you will be given some free editorial when you book an advert.

The catalogue entry

You are normally allocated a space in the catalogue to provide a short description of your company and the products or services which you are exhibiting. They normally ask for 100 to 200 words which are inserted free of charge. Try are remember to do this as early as possible. Most exhibitors leave it until the last moment and then a day or so after the deadline they quickly rush out a few sentences about the company. A good catalogue entry should include:

1 The main reason for visiting the stand.

2 A brief breakdown of the products or services on show.

3 Some background to the company if there is enough space.

4 The name of someone to contact and their telephone number.

The life of the catalogue may be much longer than just the three or four days of the show so remember to have a message that will last.

Public relations

An exhibition provides huge scope for public relations. If your company employs a PR agent then make sure they are fully briefed about the exhibition and are charged with the task of maximising the PR benefit from your participation. That is what they get paid for. If not then here are a few ideas about what you can achieve.

Before the exhibition

Most organisers now provide a list of the magazines and editors that will be covering the exhibition. If they don't, ask them to give you one. The organisers will be providing a lot of show publicity and will advise you how to get the most out of it. Read the details in the exhibitors' manual. The organisers want you to have a successful exhibition and will provide you with help in this department. They may even send out press releases and other articles direct to the magazines for you.

Having discovered which magazines are going to write about the exhibition then put together some interesting press releases which they can use. It is no good sending them a copy of your current brochure and hoping that they will turn this into an interesting story, as most editors do not have the time to do this. Look at the particular publications - every editor has his or her own style. Most magazines are divided into a number of different story lengths. If possible, calculate the appropriate length and then write a story that fits. Press releases need to be presented in an easy-to-follow way. The easier you make it for the editor the more likely you are to be involved in the publication. The basics of good press releases are as follows:

1. Send your press release on headed paper marked "Press Release". If you are rich enough then have some specially printed. Or you can create the effect using DTP and an office laser printer.

2. At the top of the press release address the release to the editor by name. Make the whole press release look as if you have specially written it for that magazine.

3. Double space the text. This makes it easy for the editor to read and edit.

4. The first paragraph should contain all the major information. Do not be tempted to start a press release with hackneyed phrases like "Jo Bloggs and Co Ltd., an old established family business with 50 years experience in the printing business...." Get straight to the point.

5. Put your name and contact number at the bottom of each page.

6. Tell the editor how long the press release is, i.e. 1,500 words. The editor knows how much space this will fill up and can plan accordingly.

7. If appropriate give him a shortened version for inclusion in his small bits column. All editors are left with 150 -200 word gaps which they have to fill with interesting information.

8. If possible send pictures. Make sure you mark up the back of the pictures in pencil to prevent show through - saying what they are and which is the top. It may be perfectly obvious to you which way up your machine is but to the poor page make-up staff it is another job which has to be done at the last moment.

9. If the information is to be used after a certain date then tell the press when they can start using it.

Make sure that you get your press releases in as soon as possible. The earlier they arrive the more likely they are to be included.

During the exhibition

The exhibition itself offers a number of opportunities to get good public relations. Firstly, there is the press office. This is normally a small area set aside for the press to meet in. The organisers provide racking and ask you to deliver your press packs to them at the start of the show. Your aim is to get your press pack in to pole position and to do this you need to enlist the help of the press officer. Go in at the start of the show and chat to the press officer. Hand over your press kit and then return each morning and afternoon of the exhibition to check that there is enough and that they are being displayed to best advantage. The press officer once he or she knows that you will keep coming back will make sure that you get a good position.

The problem with most press packs is that they all look the same. For some reason we all seem to put then in a white folder. The press are confronted with a sea of white folders most of which are hiding the exciting contents. Even the most dedicated editor will give up when confronted with so many white folders. Try and make your press pack look interesting and make it stand out from the others.

The best press pack I ever saw was done by a company selling corporate entertainment on an Island in the Midlands called Friday Island. Their press pack was a half barrel of sand with bottles in it. In each bottle was a scroll with the press message on it. Of course the press could not resist the temptation of finding out what the message in the bottle was. If your product or service does not lend itself to this kind of treatment then here are some rules about press packs.

1. Find a way of making the press pack different from all the others.

2. Put your company name at the top of front of the press pack. Some press office racks are designed to hide most of the front page of the press pack.

3. Make the information personalised. Do not just put in your company leaflets as the press will not bother to read them.

4. Put contact names and telephone numbers on every page of the press pack.

The organisers will tell you how many press packs to make up and deliver to the press office. Check that you do not run out during the exhibition.

At the end of the exhibition go and collect your press packs. You do not want your competitors to walk off with them.

Other communication during the show includes:
● Press launches. As the press are attending the exhibition it can be an ideal time to hold a press launch at the exhibition. Some organisers will provide a separate press briefing room during the exhibition for this. If you want to do a press launch on the stand then the organisers may let you do so in the evening.

● On line press information services. The advent of computers has seen the development of on line services where your press release is held on a computer data base and the press can access this without even visiting the exhibition.

● Show newspapers. At some shows the local press will do special 'show newspapers' which are given away at the exhibition. Find out if this is going to happen and then feed these local press with stories and information.

A number of organisers produce a daily exhibitors newsletter. If you have some early success at the exhibition then make sure that they know about it as they will be very pleased to write about your success. It helps them to get others to re-book space.

● Trail guides: Increasingly organisers are looking at ways of improving the services they offer exhibitors and one of these is to offer a trail guide. They highlight your stand amongst others that are worth visiting during the exhibition.

After the exhibition

Once the show is over there are a number of additional press releases that you can do. Firstly, inform the press of your success during the show. A good success story will always get written up.

If you have been well written up by the press remember to thank them. They so rarely get thanked that the next time you ask them to write you up they will be pleased to do so. If ongoing press involvement is important to your organisation then it is possibly worth taking the press out to lunch.

Advise the organisers of success stories about your stand. Send them a picture of your exhibition stand and details of the fantastic success that you had. Organisers will put this into their exhibition bulletin for next year.

Internal communications

One of the important aspects of exhibiting is the ability to motivate your staff. Your aim is to have enthusiastic, well briefed, friendly staff on your stand. The best way of achieving this is to keep them fully informed about the exhibition. This can be done through a company newsletter or if you don't have one then create a simple exhibition bulletin of your own and send it out to all the stand staff.

In advance of the show send out details of the stand and the products or services which are going to be featured.

After the show produce the good news sheet which congratulates those staff that have done par-

ticularly well. Not only does this kind of communication motivate the stand staff but it also helps to secure your exhibition budget in future years.

Leaflets

Do you really want to give away leaflets from the exhibition stand? This may sound like a daft question but when you see visitors with carrier bags of leaflets leaving the exhibition hall you have to wonder just how many of them get read.

Some companies give out leaflets like confetti from their exhibition stand in the belief that if they give away enough then some of them will lead to future business. Salespeople say they need leaflets to give away. Many use them as the opening to a conversation. The problem with giving away leaflets is:
● A visitor can collect so many that unless your leaflet is totally relevant to their needs there is little chance that it will be read after the exhibition.
● Having given the customer your leaflet it is difficult to follow-up after the exhibition. When contacted after the exhibition the visitor says that they have already got your information on file and that if they ever need your services then they will contact you.

The single major benefit of leaflets is that they can be used to get visitors off your stand.

When designing an exhibition leaflet you should consider including the following information:
● The call to action. Most leaflets produced for exhibitions are very weak when it comes to converting interest into business. You need to put on the leaflet

a very strong reason why the potential customer should contact you again after the show. The most basic is "Telephone this number for further information". Look at ways of making the call to action as strong as possible. "Use the order form below to get a 10% discount off your first order". "Apply now for further information and receive a free gift".

● Make your leaflets different from the others. Most leaflets are standard A4 in design. After the exhibition when the visitor goes through the pile of leaflets that he or she has collected at the show your leaflet will compete amongst all the other A4 leaflets. Make yours a different size so that it stands out from the crowd.

● Exhibition leaflets, like advertising, need to be written to grab the visitors attention. Keep them short and simple. Technical data can always be requested after the event.

Leaflets cost a lot of money to produce so make sure that your stand staff are aware of this and train them to treat leaflets with respect. If the customer feels that they have something of value then they are more likely to read them. Leaving piles of leaflets lying around on your stand or in leaflet dispensers projects the message that they are not of any great value.

Exhibition gifts and giveaways

Most companies feel the need to have a small gift to giveaway from the exhibition stand. The most common are the company pen and the carrier bag. There are thousands of different business gifts that you can give away. There are even exhibitions held around the country where companies exhibit such items. Below I have listed a few examples of gifts that I have seen used effectively at exhibitions.

● Carrier bags. The problem with carrier bags is that so many companies give them away and to make them have any lasting value is very difficult. One organisation produces a limited edition, very high quality, paper bag with a specially chosen historic picture on it. The bags are always very sought after by not only the visitors but by the other exhibitors. They now keep the bags at the back of the stand and only give them to potential customers.

● Logo bugs. These are little furry characters which are stuck to the lapel of the visitor. They can be used very effectively to identify the customers that you have already spoken to. They are normally very well received as people take them home to their children.

● Telephone cards. These have real value and staying power. You can now order a short run of these cards and have your logo and a personalised message on them. Customers tend to keep them in their wallets and they provide a constant reminder on your company. They are additionally collectors items and their value increases very rapidly.

● Hats, badges and balloons. For public shows these can be very effective especially if your target audience is parents as their children will drag them on to your stand in order to get the free gift.

The golden rule with free gifts is that they should

be appropriate to your company and your message. If your free gift can be tied into your product then it has a much great chance of making a lasting impression on the customer.

Video & television presentations

Companies are often tempted to show the company video from their stand. I remember the first major exhibition I ever attended in Germany. I had to stand in front of a 27 screen video wall for three days listening to a 20 minute company presentation in German. Apart from the fact that I must have looked bored beyond belief it was very difficult to stop customers because of the noise and the visual impact of the presentation.

If you have a complex message and you want to get it across using video then make sure that it is as short as possible - a maximum of four minutes. Provide a seperate area where those interested customers can go and look at the presentation.

Do not let the stand staff turn off the presentation during the exhibition as all you will be left with is a blank screen. And make sure that a company logo or other suitable graphic is displayed in the intervals between presentation screenings.

Other stand communications

● Telephone: most organisers now suggest you hire a mobile telephone during the exhibition as it is cheaper than a fixed line. If you are taking credit card transactions on the stand then you will need one for the authorisation link.

● Fax machine: this can be very useful if your aim is to follow up very quickly from the exhibition. You can fax your contact sheets through to your office during the day and then they can act on them.

● A computer link can be useful if you need access to your customer data base during the exhibition.

Exhibition communications can be seen as the icing on the cake. With a little thought and some effort you can get plenty of free publicity for your product or service. Most importantly you can influence those potential customers and get on to their shopping list which in turn will make it much easier for your stand staff to have a profitable exhibition.

Summary

● The aim is to get on as many of the visitors' "shopping list" as possible. Should you send out invitations and or carry cards?
● What advertising are you doing before, during and after the exhibition?
● Make your catalogue entry interesting, personal and lasting.
● Develop a public relations campaign.
● Leaflets. Are they really necessary or should they be saved for the follow-up after the event?
● What communications do you need on the stand?

This section concentrates on the manning and motivation of staff on an exhibition stand. Most people concentrate on the tangible aspects of exhibiting - the stand, design, graphics, etc. They spend very little time concentrating on the one aspect which will make or break the exhibition. Unlike other forms of marketing exhibitions are about people. It is often said that people buy people. Research shows that the most important factor in doing business with a company is the people with whom the buyer deals. The way your staff handle themselves on the stand which will make the difference between a good exhibition and a poor one. The problem most of us have is that we believe the staff know what they are doing and why they are there. In truth most stand staff see exhibitions as difficult and sometimes frightening experience, because we ask them to stand on a stage and perform in front of strangers. This, for most people is quite difficult to do. Stand staff rarely have performance targets, clearly set objectives or methods for measuring their success. We rely on their sales ability, normally gained from entirely different selling situations, without considering appropriate stand staff training.

In order to look at exhibitions in a positive way we need first to look at the motivation of the visitor and the problems which large numbers of visitors create when they visit an exhibition.

The visitor

Exhibitions are informal selling situations. It is neither the visitors nor the exhibitors' home ground. In 'normal' selling situations the buyer is on his home ground and to a large extent it is he who sets the agenda. All salespeople will have a story of the buyer who sits behind a large leather topped desk, with his back to the window (so you can't see the expression on his face), while the poor salesperson sits on a tiny chair below the front of his desk. However, the buyer is in a very different frame of mind. Firstly he has given up his time to attend. Secondly research shows that 78% of all visitors state that their main reason for attending exhibitions is to see what's new. Thirdly, buyers today have to justify their time. The buyer's motivation is therefore somewhat different to the normal selling situation and, consequently, you can approach him in a different, more positive, way.

He may be new to his job or indeed it may be a whole new industry to him. About one third of all visitors will be in this category. This means that a large number of visitors come with a very open frame of mind. They want to learn about new ideas and they are willing to talk to people.

An exhibition may attract a very large number of visitors from all different walks of life. Each has his own reason for being there. Examples of the types of visitor at a show includes:

Customers

Potential customers

Students

Specifiers

Technical people

Employees of your company

Competitors

The press

Complainers

People trying to sell to you

The public

The list is endless. The problem that the stand staff face is that it is very difficult to tell the good potential customers from the time wasters.

At an exhibition which attracts 10,000 visitors over three days you may be asking your stand staff to sift through as many as six customers per minute at the busy times. So how do the stand staff know which are the potential customers and which are the ones to avoid?

Classifying visitors

Visitors come in three classic groups.

The definitely interested

The definitely uninterested

The floating voters (the undecided)

It is easy to deal with the definitely interested because they march on to your stand and almost demand attention. They may not be the best people to talk to but at least they are interested. Stand staff who are having a quiet day latch on to these people and talk to them for as long as possible. But they may be existing customers who have no new business to give you. They may be time wasters who just want to pass the time finding out as much about your products and services as possible. They may even be competitors who just want to tie up your stand staff and stop them talking to the people they should really be speaking to.

With the definitely uninterested it does not matter what your stand staff do, they will not be interested in your products or services. Even if you have the most exciting stand demonstration they are not interested.

However, it is the floating voters, the people who may be interested in your proposition, who are the ones that you really want to talk to. By talking to this group of people you will pick up those vital new contacts which will turn your exhibition presence into a fantastic success.

The opportunity - and hence the problem - is that there are a large number of people at an exhibition. Visitors who in the main are looking for new ideas and new solutions to their problems. Your stand staff do not know which are good and which are bad.

Most companies who attend their first exhibition believe that the potential customers are going to walk up to their stand and leap on with their cheque book open. They may not. Firstly, they have to understand what you are and what you offer. If your stand does not explain this then it is unlikely that the visitor will stop at your stand and ask you what you are doing there. Secondly, walking onto a stand can be quite difficult especially if there are three or four stand staff waiting to pounce on them as soon as they arrive. Thirdly, the visitor may not know that what you have to offer is exactly what they want. They may need to be sold the idea.

Exhibitor's learning curve

We have developed a learning curve along which some exhibitors travel when exhibiting for the first few times. In fact some exhibitors never get past stage 1 whilst others develop excellent ways of exhibiting.

Stage 1: Passive exhibiting

When first put onto an exhibition stand, staff use this method. It is in fact the method used by most exhibitors even those who have a lot of experience. You wait until a visitor comes onto your stand and you say "Can I help you"? The answer is normally, "No thank you, I am just looking". Once this has happened a few times the stand staff tend to retreat to the back of the stand which makes it even more difficult to start a conversation. After a few hours they even prompt the answer by saying "Can I help you or were you just looking?".

The reason this method does not work is that the staff are inviting the customer to say no just by asking the simple question "Can I help you?". Look at it

from the point of view of the visitor. They have given up their time and attended the show, yet everyone greets them with the same four words.

Of course this does not put off the definitely interested visitor who really wants to talk to you; but it does stop most visitors from coming on to your stand.

By the end of the first day of the exhibition the stand staff are so demoralised that they have either taken to talking amongst themselves, or in the case of one exhibitor I saw, he had retreated to the back of the stand and spent the next two days reading his newspaper.

Some exhibitors never learn this basic lesson and they go on exhibiting by saying "Can I help you?" Use of this passive technique will still get some results and some exhibitors are happy with this low level of achievement. Other exhibitors find the whole experience too negative and give up after the first show. There are a number, however, who move onto the next stage.

Stage 2: The leaflet givers

The aim is to stop people and get them into a conversation. Having discovered that "Can I help you?" does little to achieve this aim the stand staff try the leaflet giving method. This, in it's simplest form, is standing at the edge of the stand handing out leaflets to everyone who gets within range.

It does have advantages over stage 1. There are some people who, when given a leaflet will then stop for a chat. Basically, we are all polite people and when given something for nothing we will respond to it.

The majority of people however take the leaflet and after stuffing it into the overfull carrier bag will move on. Again there is a possibility that when they get home after the exhibition they will read the leaflet and if there is something in it which they are interested in they will respond to it. But take a look at your leaflets. Are they A4 glossy leaflets? Do they look like everyone else's leaflets? Remember you are hoping that the visitor will read your leaflet just because they have had a copy thrust into their hand.

Leaflets are of course very expensive and if all you want to do is to distribute them then there are cheaper and more effective ways of doing so.

Some organisations go one step further and employ personality boys and girls to hand out the leaflets for them. This may save the stand staff time but equally one or two extra people at the front of your stand can be a very effective barrier to those more important customers who really want to get on to the stand.

Giving away leaflets from an exhibition stand can be a very expensive hobby. I remember when I was a marketing manager and I would attend an exhibition and collect all the leaflets that were offered. I would return to my office the next day and put the carrier bag of leaflets into my in-tray, with every intention of reading them. But having been away from the office for a day there would be plenty of

work and correspondence to catch up on. After about a week I would put the carrier bag, still untouched with all the leaflets in it, into my desk drawer. I still had every intention of going through it to extract the things I was most interested in. Normally, about a year later I would find the carrier bag full of leaflets and if I was very organised I would deposit it in the waste paper bin shortly before I attended next year's exhibition. This may be a cynical view of leaflets collected at an exhibition but I am sure that many people never read the leaflets you give them.

Leaflets can be used effectively to draw people on to your stand. It does however require a very well trained member of staff to stop a visitor and draw them onto the stand using a leaflet. The best use of this method I saw was a small engineering company that went to an exhibition in February each year. They had prepared some pocket diaries for the coming year and offered these to visitors as they passed the stand. As it was only February most people would accept this novel gift and the exhibitor was able to start up many a positive conversation.

Probably the best use of leaflets on an exhibition stand is to get rid of people. When you have had a conversation with someone and you want to get rid of them then a leaflet can be used as an effective sign-off.

Having tried both "Can I help you?" and leaflet giving the determined exhibitor then moves onto stage three.

Stage Three: The Free Prize draw

At every exhibition you will see an exhibitor who is running a free prize draw on his stand. We have all seen the gold fish bowl or the large box with the legend "Put your business card in here for a chance to win a bottle of champagne". The stand staff open the conversation with "would you like to win a bottle of champagne?" You give them your business card and then you are off. As a visitor to trade shows I always carry a lot of spare business cards so that I can enter as many of these draws as possible.

I have also discovered how to win! Have a business card printed with your name as the director of a major multinational company on it. It is surprising how many supposedly totally random draws you win with an impressive title.

As an exhibitor who tries the free prize draw you end up with a whole host of business cards which are unqualified leads. You don't know if they are any good or just hoping to win a bottle. If all you want from the exhibition is the names and addresses of the people that attended, then rent the list from the organisers who put on the exhibition. In some cases you do not even have to attend the show to get hold of this list. Equally, an unqualified lead means that a salesperson has to follow-up 'cold' after the exhibition. When faced with a hundred cold calls to make most salespeople give up after the first few.

Free prize draws can become very sophisticated and can produce worthwhile results. At public shows where it is not possible to get the list of visitors from the organisers then the aim may be to get as many names and addresses as possible. It may also be possible to get the visitor to fill in a small questionnaire which may then be used to get a qualified lead either at the show or afterwards as part of the follow-up.

The basic rules of a good prize draw are:
● The prize should be related to your product or service. If you are a hotel then give away a weekend break. If you manufacture cars then give away a car.
● Make sure that the entry into the prize draw is done on a separate form which asks a number of questions about the interest or lack of it that the person entering has in your products or services.
● Spread the prizes. People believe that they will never be lucky enough to win a really big prize. If there are a lot of smaller prizes then the visitor will believe that they have a greater chance. At the Incentive Marketing show the prize is quite often the incentive which the exhibitor is trying to sell. Some companies give the prize to every worthwhile lead obtained in the prize draw. The salespersons follow-up technique is to ring up the winner, announce that they have won the prize and then ask for an appointment to deliver it. This can be a cheap way of getting into target companies to make sales presentations.

Prize draws can add a lot of fun and interest to your exhibition stand but they must be used to achieve your exhibition aims and not just something to do on the stand.

In an attempt to further improve the number of qualified sales leads the now seasoned exhibitor moves on to the fourth part of the learning curve.

Stage Four: The competition

This is really just an extension of the free prize draw but used correctly, it can act as a big draw to your stand. The easiest and probably most overused version of this is the putting competition. You create a small putting green on the stand and then you invite visitors to try their luck. During the time it takes the customer to perform the task the salesperson is able to ask a few questions about their interest in the exhibition. There are many examples of this type of competition including:

Knocking tins off a shelf with bean bags.
Throwing table tennis balls into goldfish bowls.
Dice rolling games.
Card games.

They work because they get people to stop and try. They often fail because there is no link between them and the proposition that you are selling. The real skill with competitions is to make the competition fit your company and the products/services which you are selling.

Having a busy stand is the single most important way of attracting additional people onto your stand. This is effectively a variation on the 'building an edge' technique from street marketing.

There used to be a street market stall holder that started each day by holding up an 80 piece dinner service. He would offer this dinner service at £80, then £69, then £40. All the way down in price to £1. By this stage he would have a couple of hundred people stand around the stall waving their arms in the air shouting for the chance to buy this dinner service for just £1. He would then smash the whole dinner service on the ground. He would then hold up a tea service or similar and sell it for £15.

The aim is to draw a crowd of people onto or around the stand so that your stand staff have a chance to talk to them. Once the visitor sees a busy stand he will be more inclined to come and look at what is going on. Nobody likes to be the first on to the stand - yet we are all happy to form a queue or join the crowd.

When looking at competitions it is important to balance the activity against the number of people who are going to be attracted to it and the number of stand staff available to talk to the visitors. There is little point in getting a crowd of a hundred or so visitors when there are only a couple of stand staff to deal with them.

Stage Five: Demonstrations and stand activities

Visitors to exhibitions are always interested in watching demonstrations. Recent figures show that 87% of visitors see demonstrations as the most important advantage an exhibition has over other forms of marketing.

In the computer industry this takes the form of

software/hardware demonstrations which may result in the exhibitor building a theatre on the stand with seating and a formal 20 minute presentation every half hour. Some computer companies go to extraordinary lengths to get you to sit and watch their demonstration. They give away hats, pens, badges and free software if you sit and listen to them. Some companies are very good at it, employing professional presenters who provide more than just a demonstration but a stage show which is worth watching just for the presentation itself.

Stand activities can be even more effective if you can get the visitor to participate in the demonstration. At a bakery show one company was asking the bakers to fill a meringue shell using a piping bag. Every baker in the country can do this: after all they do it every day. However, the attraction of being able to do it on the stand and demonstrate to their friends and colleagues that they were good at it was just too much and there were bakers queuing in the aisles to have a go.

If you can demonstrate your product/service or idea in a way which lets the visitor participate, then you are sure to stop a lot of additional visitors. A trade journal who had a stand at the exhibition they organised had a hospitality stand. They were selling to a very well defined customer base who were in fact the exhibitors at the exhibition. They had arranged for a cartoonist to be on their stand during the exhibition and they invited all their major customers onto the stand to have a cartoon drawn of them. Once the cartoon was drawn it was displayed on the stand which added to the appeal of the stand. At the end of the show they had the cartoons framed and then sent them to the customers as something to keep. I've still got mine.

The ideas for stand demonstrations above all have their merits and weaknesses. There are many companies who are either too small or have a product that does not lend itself to this treatment so a number of organisations have developed a method for approaching the customer which we call Positive Professional Canvassing

Stage Six: Positive Professional Canvassing

Let's start by saying what Positive Professional Canvassing is *not*. Everyone has seen the canvassers in the high street and knows how to avoid them. They stand with a folder in the middle of the street and if you see them ahead of you you try and pass them by on the other side of the street. At an exhibition the visitor is in an entirely different frame of mind. The visitor is there to find out new information and look at new ideas. The visitor is very open, he or she wants to talk to people and is therefore very approachable.

The aim of the exhibition stand is to provide an opportunity to talk to as many people as possible, to sort the good from the bad and to talk to the people who may be interested in your products if approached in the right way.

The aim of the stand staff is to get visitors on to the stand and to build a lively and inviting stand which will encourage additional visitors to stop.

Positive Professional Canvassing achieves this in a number of different ways. Firstly, it gives your stand staff a positive job to do on the stand while there are no visitors on it. Secondly, it provides stand staff with a professional way of opening the conversation. Thirdly, by giving the stand staff something to do during the day, the time does not drag, they do not become bored or restless, they are - and appear to be - more positive approachable people.

There is a rule which appears in most exhibitors' manuals which says that you shall not canvass in the aisles at exhibitions. The aim of this rule is to stop exhibitors and other people from roaming around the exhibition stopping people in the aisles. Positive Professional Canvassing is not like this at all and no one who has ever tried it has been prevented from carrying on.

How does it work?

The stand staff have a small A5 clip board which gives them the status to stop and ask people. From the edge of the stand they start the conversation with the standard greeting "Good morning, Can I ask you a couple of questions?".

95% of people say "yes". For those who say "no" (there are always a few) the stand staff say "Thank you. Have a good exhibition". It is worth noting that the ones who say no are almost always the people you do not want to speak to. They are either the people who have no right to be in the exhibition or they may even be the type of visitor who is really a salesman that is trying to sell to the exhibitors. Whoever they are, as professional canvassers your staff need to be polite and to end the conversation in a positive way.

The 95% who say "yes" can now be asked a couple of closed questions. Remember at this stage that 80% of exhibitors have asked them "Can I help you?", to which they have replied "No thank you, I am just looking". To have an exhibitor start the conversation in a positive and professional way is very refreshing. I have even had visitors say "Yes please. You are the first person to speak to me. I thought there was something wrong with me".

What is a closed question and why canvass in this way? A closed question is one which requires a yes or no answer. The aim of the canvassing is to sort out the potential customers. The stand staff need to establish if this visitor is worth talking to and therefore a couple of closed questions can be used to find out if the visitor is a potential customer.

Simple closed questions are used. Do you buy widgets? Do you buy from our company? You need to devise the questions which the staff are going to use. Better still, if you are having a briefing meeting then get them to come up with their own questions. You are asking the canvassers to stop and greet people all day during the exhibition and it is far better if they come up with their own questions because they

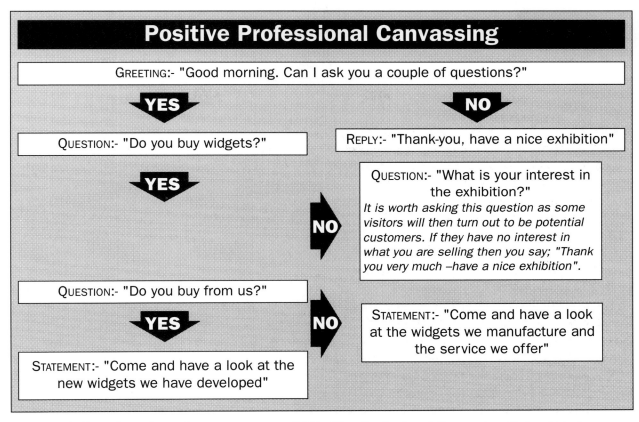

Positive Professional Canvassing

GREETING:- "Good morning. Can I ask you a couple of questions?"

YES

NO

QUESTION:- "Do you buy widgets?"

REPLY:- "Thank-you, have a nice exhibition"

YES

QUESTION:- "What is your interest in the exhibition?"
It is worth asking this question as some visitors will then turn out to be potential customers. If they have no interest in what you are selling then you say; "Thank you very much –have a nice exhibition".

NO

QUESTION:- "Do you buy from us?"

YES

NO

STATEMENT:- "Come and have a look at the widgets we manufacture and the service we offer"

STATEMENT:- "Come and have a look at the new widgets we have developed"

This simple flow chart shows the steps to successful Positive Professional Canvassing. It should to be tailored to suit the products, services or ideas that you are trying to exhibit. Before the exhibition get your stand staff to practice this canvassing technique so that they are comfortable with it when the exhibition starts.

will sound more natural.

The questions need to be aimed at sorting out the visitors you want to talk to - your target group of visitors. If you are looking to sell additional ideas to existing customers then the questions are easy and about identifying your customers. If you are looking for new customers then you need to find out if they buy your products at all. If you are selling ideas or services then the questions may be more general. It does not matter what is your reason for exhibiting. With a bit of thought you will easily be able to develop a couple of questions which are suitable to the audience that you are trying to find.

The object is to sort the good from the bad, the wheat from the chaff. Positive Professional Canvassing gives you a method for doing this which is fast, professional and, above all, a very successful technique.

Once you have found a visitor who shows an interest in your proposition then the next stage is to get their name and address etc. Prepare a form for doing this., an example shown here. It is important that you train all your stand staff to get this information before they show the visitors the product or service because it is much easier to do so at this point rather than at the end of the interview.

After getting the customers' details the next stage is to show the customers the products and to do the selling from the stand. Work out with your stand staff the number of people you want them to talk to each day of the exhibition and this will give you an idea about how long they should spend selling to them. In our experience stand staff are likely to spend far too long talking to a single visitor and you need to impress on them that they should talk to as many customers and potential customers as possible.

At the end of the conversation it is important that the stand staff tell the visitor what is going to happen next, what follow-up, to expect. You may be going to call them to arrange a meeting, or to send them some further information. What ever the follow-up the stand staff need to tell the visitor so that when the follow-up occurs the visitor is expecting it.

Contact Sheet

Name

Title

Company

Address

Telephone   Fax

Canvassing Questions

1 Do you use widgets?   Tick box

2 Do you buy from us?   ☐

If no who is your current supplier   ☐

New products demonstrated

1 Super Widgets

2 New Blue Widgets   ☐
                                                      ☐

Follow-up agreed

Send further information   ☐

Phone for appointment   ☐
                                                      ☐

Comments

Completed by

Day

                                          Interest level
                                          A   B   C   D

After the visitor has left the stand the staff should mark each contact sheet with a letter A, B, C or D. 'A' means 'Red hot prospect worth follow-up up, this customer will give us the business'.

'B' meaning 'Good prospect worth follow-up'. 'C' meaning 'Poor' and D meaning 'Dump. This customer was a waste of time'.

The reason for doing this is that after the show you are able to prioritise the exhibition contacts and give the people who are doing the follow-up some idea of the good ones. Of course this is just a gut reaction by the stand staff but if they are able to indicate which prospects are the good ones so that when it comes to doing the follow-up there is a chance of early success.

Positive Professional Canvassing produces real benefits to the stand staff when manning the stand. It gives them something to do when there is no one on the stand. It gives them a system and the words for approaching the visitor.

Remember that we are all a little shy when it comes to talking to people we have never met before and positive canvassing helps stand staff to get over this shyness. Once you have got a number of visitors on to your stand you do not have to canvass any more because the visitor will naturally gravitate to a busy stand.

Very few companies practice Positive Professional Canvassing so that you can be sure that you will be one of only a very select few who try it. The results are fantastic: companies who we have trained in this approach increase their number of qualified exhibition leads by a factor of between 5 and 10 times. Please give it a go and let us know what effect it has on your exhibiting.

Stand staff motivation

Most companies run a briefing meeting for the stand staff. At it's simplest it is a quick chat about tactics just before the exhibition opens. The more professional companies get their staff together for a full blown training session prior to the exhibition. We have listed below an agenda with brief notes.

Stand objectives.
Tell them why you are exhibiting, how much it is costing and what the key objectives/aims of the exhibition are.

Product/service briefing
If you are selling a number of different products/ideas from the stand then make sure that the stand staff are fully briefed. There is nothing worse than a member of the stand staff being unable to answer even the basic questions about a product. If you are using hospitality people on the stand then make sure that they are also briefed.
On a stand which has lots of different very technical products then it may be necessary to have specialists. Brief the staff to guide visitors to these specialists and make the specialists stay on the stand during the exhibition.

Communications
Give your staff a run through of the public relations that has happened prior to the exhibition opening. Show them copies of the adverts you have placed

and the invitations that you have sent out.

Practical matters

It is important that stand staff are fully conversant with the housekeeping practical matters that makes their day go smoothly. If they know about and are confident of the arrangements, they won't have to spend precious exhibition time worrying about whether there is enough time to catch the train home. A list of such topics would include:

Tea breaks & location of toilets
Hotels and travel arrangements
Position of stand/stand no.
Stand telephone number
Lunch arrangements
Dress requirements

Staff rota

To get the best out of your stand staff you need to give them time off during the exhibition. Some exhibitions are always at their busiest at lunch time so it may not be appropriate to give the stand staff time off then. We have found the best work to rest ratio to be two hours working on the stand and then half an hour off.

When staff have a rest period they should be encouraged to leave the stand. Some organisers arrange a special lounge area for exhibitors' staff. If possible encourage the stand staff to leave the exhibition hall and go out into the fresh air during the rest breaks.

Stand manager

Appoint a stand manager and make sure that he/she has the authority to do the job. Stand managers need the authority to throw their Managing Director off the stand during the show. The duties of the stand manager are to make sure that the stand is properly manned during the exhibition. On a large stand at the beginning of the day it may be necessary to reduce the stand staff so that the visitors are not overwhelmed by eager salespeople. A stand manager needs to have the authority to do this. Equally, the stand manager is the person who will deal with the press and other odd people who arrive at the stand.

A stand manager is also responsible for collecting the sales enquiry forms during the day and keeping track of the performance of individual salespeople.

Complainers

Once in a while even the best companies in the world get a complainer on their stand. It is potentially the worst position that the stand staff can be put in. So you need to have prepared a system for dealing with the complainers before the show.

The first thing to do is to look at it from the complainer's point of view. In the UK we are not very good at complaining. We do not like to complain. We certainly do not like to complain in public. So a complainer who comes to your stand to air his/her grievance against the company is someone who has thought long and hard about their complaint. They deserve to be treated in the best possible way.

From the company's point of view you do not want other customers, competitors and the press seeing a complainer on your stand. Therefore, job one is to get the complainer off the stand. You may have a private seating area on the stand and you could also use this to take the complainer away from the visible part of the stand. If you manage to get the complainer off the stand then remove your exhibitor badge and take them off for a drink or a cup of coffee.

It may be necessary to produce the 'boss' to deal with the complaint. The member of your staff who is the best at dealing with complaints can be given a very senior title and stand staff can pass the complainer on to them. Complainers think they are getting somewhere when they talk to the 'boss'.

Finally, develop a help system. Have a signal like fingers crossed behind your back to alert other stand staff that you need help. This is also useful when getting rid of time wasters.

Recording leads

Go through the sales contact sheet or sales enquiry form. Remember to ask them to put A,B,C, or D after they have finished talking to the visitor. Get the staff to hand the enquiry forms to the stand manager during the exhibition. In many cases these forms represent the whole reason for being at the exhibition. They need to be rounded up or they will get lost, or even worse, stolen by your competitors. Some stand staff like to hold on to the enquiry forms so that they can follow-up the contact after the exhibition themselves. So a rigid system for collecting them during the exhibition helps.

The stand manger should check each enquiry sheet as soon as he receives it from the salesperson. He can check that all the information has been gathered properly and that it is legible. If the stand manager finds bits missing then he can ask the salesperson for clarification straight away. Trying to get stand staff to remember a particular customer at the end of the day after they have spoken to a few hundred people is impossible.

The score chart

Once you have set a target for the exhibition, break the target down into daily targets and for a big stand into hourly targets. If your target is to get 150 qualified leads during the exhibition then the daily target may be 50 for the first day 60 for the busy second day and 40 for the last day. Draw a simple score chart showing the salespeople's names and then as they hand in there contact sheets mark their scores up on the chart. By doing this you can let the stand staff know how they are doing during the day. It acts as very good motivation for stand staff as well. No one likes to be last in the company and there are a number of people who will always strive to win these competitions.

At one exhibition I saw my boss, the Commercial Director, who did not really believe in exhibitions.

The company was a very old established business in a very traditional industry. He thought that we knew every potential customer and that they all knew who we were. Using the canvassing and scoring techniques we found 586 potential new customers who had never heard of us. Towards the end of the exhibition I caught the Commercial Director stopping old friends of his and asking them to give him an order so that he could fill in a few enquiry forms. Even the boss didn't want to be the last on the score chart.

Daily briefings

Arrange a daily briefing both at the start and end of each day of the show. In order to get all the staff to attend on time Microsoft provide bacon sandwiches and coffee an hour before the show started. The object is to go through the daily targets and rota so that all the staff are ready to start the day in a positive way.

If you are running the score-chart system then at the end of each day you can arrange a small presentation to the staff who have done the best during the day. One GEC company decided to do this and they gave a small cuddly hedgehog to the top three salesmen each day. On the second day I saw one of the salesmen working very hard. He had already won the prize the day before but was determined to win again the second day. The reason for his enthusiasm was not that he wanted to be the top salesman but that he had two children and he needed two hedgehogs to take home with him.

On another stand we awarded 'the golden yo-yo'. The staff were giving away cheap plastic yo-yos as a free gift to the customers and we spray painted a few of these and attached them to cheap frames bought from Woolworth's. The salespeople were so pleased with these awards that even today 6 years later you can still find them hanging up in the salesmen's offices.

The principle of the prize is not that it should be of any great value, both the toy hedgehog and the golden yo-yo's cost only a few pounds each, but that the prize is recognition of a job well done. If you have salespeople who do really well at the exhibition then why not get the boss to send them a letter congratulating them or publish the results in the company newsletter.

Exhibitions are hard work

Ask anyone who has ever worked on an exhibition and they will tell you that it is very hard work. Head Office staff tend to think that the exhibition is just an excuse for a party but working a stand can be very demanding. The worst form of exhibiting is when you have nothing to do and no one to speak to. Stand staff who stand and watch the visitors pass the stand all day long are always the ones who suffer the most. Of course if your stand staff have been trained to canvass the visitors then they will find that the day passes very much more quickly.

Some companies suffer from the work hard play hard philosophy which means that the night before the exhibition when they are in the hotel they stay up and have a very long party. The reason that exhibition staff have that white faced appearance is not the bright lights. It is just straight alcohol poisoning and lack of sleep. It really shows when you have to work on an exhibition stand all day. If you really need your staff to have a big party at the exhibition then it is worth booking them in for an extra night at the end of the show and letting them have a really good time.

The other major problem with exhibitions is that the exhibition halls are usually very hot and dry environments, caused by the mass of people the bright lights and the air conditioning systems used to heat exhibition halls. This results in stand staff losing a large volume of water. An estimate of the water loss is between one and two litres a day. In addition to this the stand staff may be suffering from the effects of dehydration due to alcohol and compounding this is the thick caffeine-rich coffee which they always seem to brew at exhibitions.

This physically makes the joints ache, especially the legs which are being additionally punished by being stood on all day. The solution to this problem is to drink lots of plain mineral water during the exhibition and it is worth having a supply of it on the stand.

Comfortable shoes are a must but equally it seems that shoes are one of the first things that the visitors notice about a salesperson's appearance and therefore they need to be smart and polished.

Body language

The problem with working on an exhibition stand is that is is very simple to fall into a number of body language traps. Standing on the edge of the stand with your arms folded creates a huge barrier to potential visitors. Similarly standing with hands behind your back merely shows that you are waiting for something better to do. To avoid these traps, stand staff should have a clipboard or something similar to hold.

Dress code for exhibitions

The overriding rule is that it should be appropriate to the visitor you wish to speak to and the industry you are in. Once when working on a stand in the clothing industry I was surprised at how formally the salespeople needed to dress. The salesmen all had smart suits with well tied ties and handkerchief in their breast pockets. In the computer industry it seems appropriate to wear polo shirts and smart trousers.

Major banks and department stores tend to insist on their staff wearing the company uniform, which helps to enforce the corporate message.

If you are thinking of having a stand staff uniform for the first time then a word of warning. It can stir up great passion within the company. A few years ago the catering staff at the NEC were given new uniforms to wear. The staff took an instant dislike to them and decided that they looked like convicts uniforms. To get their message of disapproval across to the management they wrote their employee numbers onto a bit of Sellotape and stuck it on the offending clothing. They then explained their disapproval to all the customers. If you want to produce a staff uniform then make sure you consult the people who have to wear it before you order it.

People buy people
When briefing the stand staff some of the hardest messages to get across are the ones which involve personal habits. When doing in house training seminars we are often asked to approach these issues because it is easier for an outsider to tackle them.

The basic principle is that 'People buy people' and you need to make your staff as acceptable as possible to the visitors they are going to talk to.

Over 60% of the population now do not smoke. More than 40% actively object to people smoking around them. So it makes common sense to have a no smoking policy on the stand. In most industries this no-smoking policy is already well established. The exception, which proves the rule, is the food industry where you still see many exhibitors smoking even when there is fresh food on their stand.

Drinking is one of the big hazards at exhibitions. Many people see hospitality at exhibitions as an important part of the exercise and this may mean building a bar on the stand. It is all too easy to have a quick drink early in the day especially if you have been up late drinking with the lads the night before. The problem is that the effect of alcohol is either to make one go to sleep or to make you more aggressive. Ask yourself, would you buy from someone who smells of drink?

Another negative effect of drinking on the stand is that it can put off the visitor, who, seeing the stand staff drinking, thinks that they are too busy to be approachable.

Be aware of lingering odours! Garlic snails and vindaloo curries the night before an exhibition can destroy your chances of success. Equally, the salesmen that prepares himself by getting out a large bucket of aftershave and dunking his head into it repeatedly can be equally off-putting.

In an ideal world all stand staff will get a good nights sleep prior to working on an exhibition stand, but then we don't live in an ideal world.

Exhibition techniques summary
- Your staff are the most important part of your exhibition. Time and money spent training and motivating will give you the best results.
- The visitor is looking for *new* ideas, products and services. He is on neutral ground and in a positive frame of mind. One third will be new to their job or new to the industry so don't assume that they will know about you, your company or your message.
- The problem with exhibitions is that there are a large number of visitors with many different interests. Your staff need to quickly establish the potentially good ones from the time wasters.

- How are your staff going to approach the visitor?
  - Passively. "Can I help you?"
  - Leaflet givers
  - Free prize draw
  - Stand competitions
  - Demonstrations
  - Positive professional canvassing
- Stand staff motivation (The staff briefing)
  - Aims & objectives
  - Product/service briefing
  - Communications
  - Practical matters
  - Staff rota
  - Stand manager
  - Complainers
  - Recording leads
  - The score chart
  - Daily briefings
- Exhibitions are hard work
  - Drink lots of water
  - Dress code for stand
  - People buy people

Exhibition follow-up is the fulfilment of the promise the stand staff made on the stand. Over 70% of companies fail to follow-up effectively after the exhibition. The reason is that they have failed to develop a campaign of follow-up after the show. Why? Because the organising of the exhibition has taken up all their time and because there is a belief that the follow-up will happen naturally. Without an effective follow-up campaign you might as well have not bothered going to the exhibition.

A large American company had an exhibition stand that it used to send over once a year to the UK for an exhibition. Part of the stand had a small lockable cabinet in it. The second year it was sent over the staff opened the cabinet and found a small box labelled "exhibition contact forms". Inside were the contact forms from the previous year.

Another company I trained in the use of Positive Professional Canvassing increased the number of qualified exhibition leads from 75 to 673. The sales manager was so impressed that three months later he invited me to lunch. When I arrived at his office the whole pile of 673 exhibition leads were still sitting on the corner of his desk.

I know that the above examples are the exception rather than the rule. However, I am convinced that most companies fail to capitalise on the exhibition enquiries that they get from the exhibition.

A number of organisations do not need to do any follow up after the exhibition. If you are selling ideas or trying to change attitudes to the general public then it may not be practical to follow up after the exhibition. If your presence at the exhibition fulfils your exhibition aims and you do not need to follow-up then you can safely ignore the rest of this chapter. For those of you who have aims which mean that you need to follow-up after the exhibition then read on.

If your staff said that you will write a letter and send them further details then that is the follow-up that the customer expects. If you promised to ring for an appointment then again that is what has to happen. When briefing your staff you will have decided what the appropriate follow-up will be. You now need to develop a plan which makes this happen.

Principles of follow-up

1. The faster the follow-up the more effective it will be. A wholesale company wanted to demonstrate that it had the most efficient delivery service in the market. On the stand they trained the stand staff to sell a low cost new product which would have wide appeal to their customers. Having got the orders on the stand they then sent them via a computer link to the local depots. This was done from the exhibition stand as soon as the orders were received. Their local depots were told to deliver the orders as soon as possible and if it meant that the manager had to put them in his car and deliver them himself so be it. They took over 700 orders on the stand and 90% of them were delivered within 12 hours. Over 50% were delivered before the visitor returned from the stand. This helped the company demonstrate that it was the fastest delivery company in the market.

2. Personalise it. On the stand you have taken the time and trouble to get the persons name, job title and address. Make sure that the follow-up is as personalised as possible. There is little point in sending out an unpersonalised mail shot as you have lost all the advantage you gained from the exhibition. One of the ways of organising fast personalised follow-up is to post the follow-up letters from the exhibition stand. All you need is a computer and someone to sit in a little office on the stand processing the letters as soon as the contact sheets are completed. The visitor will receive very few follow-up letters and is likely to remember the first one he received.

3. Go for early success. If you have asked your stand staff to mark on the contact sheet 'A', 'B', 'C' or 'D' where 'A' means red hot contact etc. then you can go through the contact sheets and sort out all the 'A' contacts. By doing this you can give your field sales staff the good ones to go after first. Salespeople can be very sceptical about the quality of sales leads generated from any form of marketing, especially exhibitions. By giving them the best ones to go after first you are giving them the ones that are most likely to

turn into business. If they have some early success with these then they are more likely to do the rest of the follow-up.

4. Don't assume that it will happen. Many companies make the mistake of sending out the contact sheets at the end of the exhibition and then never asking for any feedback afterwards. It is human nature that if you do not ask for feedback then you are unlikely to get it. Ask every person who is involved in the follow-up to give you feedback about each of the contact sheets that you have sent them.

Developing a follow-up plan

Some companies selling expensive capital machinery may not be able to attribute the sale to the exhibition stand. It may indeed be a combination of factors that eventually leads to a sale, one of which will have been the way the potential customer has been treated on the stand.

By developing a follow-up plan you can monitor the progress towards such sales which may take anything up to a couple of years to come to fruition.

If at first you don't succeed. Of all the contacts you make at the exhibition only a few will turn in to instant business. For a number of reasons the person you met at the exhibition stand may not be in a position to buy your product or service immediately after the exhibition. You have however invested both time and money in meeting and talking to these people. If your first follow-up does not bear fruit then do not throw away the contact sheet. Keep the names and addresses and then follow-up again in six months time. Some people take a little more time to convince than others.

The most common forms of follow-up are:
Letter - Telephone - Fax - Delivery - Visit

Your exhibition aims will dictate how you are going to follow-up after the exhibition.

Evaluation

We might have had a whole chapter devoted to the evaluation of exhibition stands but in principle they are very easy to measure. That is if you have set measurable objectives for your exhibition. Having read this book you will of course be setting measurable objectives for your exhibitions in the future.

We need to consider why we need to evaluate exhibitions. The principle reason is to see how cost effective they are when measured against other forms of marketing. The research shows that trade exhibitions provide a particularly good opportunity for meeting new people, launching new products and developing a strong corporate image. Public shows can provide a good platform for actually selling products. It is of course very easy to measure the success of an exhibition when you have actually taken money on the stand.

Evaluation of exhibitions becomes much harder when you are not selling products or looking for customers and distributors. Many organisations go to exhibitions to communicate messages. If you are involved in placing advertisements then you may have experienced a similar problem. There is no clear cut way to measure the effectiveness of your message communication at an exhibition. You may decide to have some market research done. This can be conducted at the time of the exhibition. You employ a market research company to interview visitors leaving the exhibition and ask them if they saw your stand and if they can remember the message. Equally, this can be done by post after the exhibition is over. One company we trained measured the number of conversations that the stand staff had on the stand. By doing this they were able to gauge the number of people they had spoken to and thus the cost per person of speaking to them. When this was compared to the cost of generating interest through advertising it was found that exhibitions were indeed a more cost effective method of marketing.

Finally, your evaluation helps you to justify your spend at exhibitions and that in turn may lead to increased exhibition budgets in future years.

Summary

- 70% of companies fail to follow-up effectively after the exhibition.
- You need to plan your follow-up campaign well in advance of the show.
- A faster follow-up is more likely to be successful..
- Personalised follow-up is essential for success.
- Good follow-up allows you to evaluate your exhibition performance and helps you to get bigger exhibition budgets in subsequent years.

The purpose of preparing a budget for an exhibition may seem obvious. However it is very difficult to forecast all the costs associated with an exhibition. The reason for leaving this chapter until the later part of the book is that we have hopefully covered enough ground to allow you to prepare a reasonable budget for your exhibitions.

Key areas

There are six key areas to consider when preparing your exhibition budget and these are.
- The cost of the space
- Services to the stand
- Stand design
- Graphics costs
- Communication and advertising costs
- Staff costs

Most exhibitors spend the majority of their money on the first four items and very little on the last two. Before setting your budget go back to your aims and consider how much you need to spend on your staff and the communications element of your exhibition spend prior to fixing any budgets. If your aim is to get as many new people onto your stand as possible then you may be better spending a larger proportion of your budget on the communications and advertising elements rather than on a larger space and more expensive stand.

If you intend to get your staff to canvass from the exhibition stand then the best investment you can make will be in staff training. If on the other hand your principal aim is to get over a strong corporate message then you will need to spend a higher proportion on your graphics costs.

On *page 74* is a simple budget schedule which you can use for the preparation of your budgets. I have listed below the key items and a brief note about each. When preparing a budget please remember to allow a contingency amount to cover the items you forget when preparing your budget.

Stand space

This is the cost of the space. If you are buying the shell scheme then it will include a number of the following items. If on the other hand if you are buying space only then you may have to budget for them.

Services to the stand

These are normally supplied by nominated contractors. Of all the services that are mentioned in the exhibitors manual the only ones which you have to use are the electrical contractors and the suppliers of water and waste services. It may be possible to make some savings on the others by shopping around.

Electrical installation. Book about a month prior to the show. Details will be provided in the

Exhibition Budget

Item	Budget	Actual	+/-
STAND SPACE			
SERVICES TO THE STAND			
Electrical Installation			
Lighting			
Water & Waste			
Gas			
Lifting services			
Insurance			
STAND DESIGN			
Design			
Building			
Transport			
Dismantling			
Storage			
Carpeting and ceilings			
Additions to Shell Scheme			
Furniture Hire			
Floral Hire			
STAND GRAPHICS			
Graphic design			
Print and Production			
Application to stand			
Transport and storage			
COMMUNICATION & ADVERTISING			
Literature design & print			
Press Packs			
Catalogue Advertising			
General advertising			
Poster & in-hall adverts			
Invitations & Carry cards			
Hospitality costs			
Photography			
Telephone			
STAFF			
Training			
Travel & Parking			
Accommodation			
Stand staff food			
Uniforms			
Staff badges			
Staff prizes			
Outside staff			
CONTINGENCY			
TOTAL			

exhibitors' manual.

Lighting. Usually bookable on the above form. However, if you have your own lights then all you will need to order is the electrical installation.

Water and waste. If you require a sink on the stand then you will need water and waste. If your requirement is for a very little supply then you can purchase or hire a unit with it's own integral water and waste system. This can be a lot cheaper than having connections in to the halls mains. If you are preparing food on the exhibition stand then you need to comply with the current health and safety environmental health regulations. The exhibition organiser will be able to advise you about this.

Gas or compressed air. Again this can be organised through the nominated contractor.

Lifting services. If you require a fork lift truck to unload your equipment then make sure that you book the service in advance. Most lifting contractors also offer storage services for empty crates during the exhibition.

Insurance. Check your company insurance. It probably covers you for third party damage at an exhibition. It is unlikely to cover your displays. If you have valuable equipment on the stand then it may be worth taking out additional insurance. Most exhibition manuals give details of an insurance firm.

Stand design
Design In today's economic climate most exhibition designers will prepare outline designs at no initial costs. However, if you ask your designer to prepare a number of designs for a forthcoming exhibition then there may be a charge.

Building Most exhibition builders will give you a fixed price for the building and dismantling of your exhibition stand.

Transport Remember to include the costs of transporting your display items and literature to the stand. At certain exhibition halls you may need to pay for parking during loading and unloading of your display items.

Dismantling/Storage
If you have a large stand then you may have to pay storage charges while the stand is in storage.

Carpeting and ceilings
Additions to shell scheme
Furniture hire
Floral hire

Stand graphics
We have identified this as a separate item because in a lot of cases graphics are produced by a different firm than the stand. Equally the graphics may be used at a number of different events.
- Graphic design
- Print and production
- Application to stand
- Transport and storage of graphics

Communications and advertising costs
- Literature design and print costs

Exhibition Planning Chart

Stand Number	Exhibition		Dates			

Item	Pre Show activity in weeks/days	Show Open	Post Show Activity	Notes

- Press packs
- Catalogue advertising
- General advertising
- Poster & in-hall advertising costs
- Invitations and carry cards
- Gifts and giveaways
- Hospitality costs
- Photography
- Telephone

Staff

- Staff training. Are you arranging a briefing meeting prior to the exhibition? If so you may need to include the cost of hiring a training room and paying for additional staff travelling costs.

- Staff travel
- Staff accommodation
- Stand staff food
- Uniforms
- Staff badges
- Staff prizes
- Outside staff
- Parking charges

One of the fundamental principles of exhibiting is that costs rise the closer you get to an exhibition. It is not only worth preparing a budget for your exhibition but also preparing a time plan so that you keep on top of all the items. This way you will avoid the last minute panics that really add to your overall costs. Shown above is a simple planning chart which you may find of use when preparing yours.

We have mentioned throughout the book that there are a lot of companies, especially the smaller exhibitors, who will benefit from the 'Do it yourself' approach to exhibiting. This approach usually means that you will need to purchase a 'system' type stand. There are very many to choose from and we have listed below the principle types which you may like to consider.

If you are intending to go down this path then there are a couple of items which you need to consider before you buy a stand. Firstly, exhibition organisers will normally offer the smaller exhibitor a shell scheme stand. As we have mentioned before this will cost you as much as £40 per square metre extra. What you get for this is the walls, a facia board, carpet and possibly some lighting or power supply. If it is then your intention to put up a system inside the shell scheme then you may be able to save money by buying space only. Some organisers dislike selling the smaller exhibitor space only. They argue that without the shell scheme the stands tend to look untidy.

The reason for wanting you to buy space only is that they make money from doing so. The problem you face by buying space only is that you will have to provide your own floor covering. This can be done by either purchasing some carpet tiles or by buying some cheap carpet and throwing it away at the end of the exhibition. Alternatively you can hire carpet from the nominated carpet contractor.

There are many different types of exhibition system available from the very small type which will fit into a small carrying case for easy transport to systems which can be developed into full blown exhibition stands. The problem with systems is that you are buying something which is available to everyone else and there is a danger that you will be unable to make your stand look different and appealing. But it will stand out from the shell scheme.

All exhibition systems are basically a method for producing a backdrop on which you can fix your own message. The salesmen of all systems will try and sell you the particular benefits of their system but bear in mind that all you are really buying is a back-drop. It is your message, graphics and displays which are really going to do the selling for you.

Benefits of exhibition systems:
● **Ease of transportation**. Most systems will pack down to a very small size and be very easy to transport. You can normally buy carrying cases to transport them in.
● **Easy to erect**. Although a couple of the more complicated systems require a masters degree in DIY, the majority of systems can be erected and dismantled very easily.

● **The ability to add to your system**. With some of the systems it is very easy to add additional panels and other features to your stand. In this way you can start with a small stand and then as your budget permits you can increase the size of it.

● **Choice of finishes.** Most major manufacturers will be able to offer you a very wide choice of finishes from the standard 'Expoloop' material which allows you to attach graphics with 'Velcro', to full colour picture panels.

Types of system stand

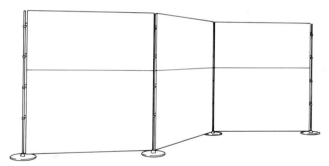

Permanent and semi-permanent displays
There are a number of simple systems for permanent and semi-permanent displays made from larger panels which are either fixed together or form part of the traditional pole and panel systems. They are ideal for use in museums, showrooms etc. They can also be used as portable exhibition systems but you may require a bigger vehicle to transport them.

The key advantage to these systems is that they give you large areas on which to display your products or graphics. They are normally finished with 'Expoloop' so that the latter can be simply attached to it.

Pop-up systems

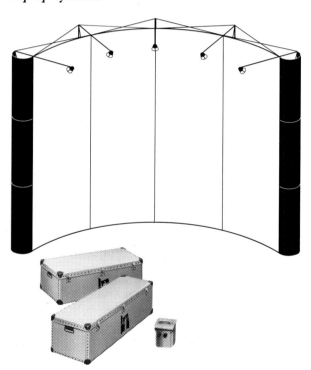

As the name implies this type of system is probably the quickest and easiest of all the systems to erect. A tubular hinged metal frame is supplied which when 'popped-up' forms the frame on which to hang the graphics panels.

The graphics panels can either be supplied covered in 'Expoloop' or a pre-finished full colour graphic or photographic panels. The system was originally invented for the American market.

It is very light weight making it very easy to transport by air. One of the great advantages with the pop-up systems is that they can give a seamless appearance to your stand, making it extremely attractive.

You can purchase a wide range of different sizes and configurations to suit your particular needs. It is also possible to purchase integral lighting systems for the system.

Simple panel systems

This are made from pre-joined panels in either sets of three or four. You purchase the number of sets you require and then place them one on top of the other to produce the size you require. You can add kickstrip panels at the bottom and header panels at the top to enhance the display. Normally the panels are finished with 'Expoloop', which is a material finish that comes in a wide range of colours and to which graphics can be attached using 'Velcro' type material.

At the end of the exhibition the panels pack down into a small portable size which will fit into the back of a family car.

Additionally you can purchase shelves for the system and lights to enhance the appearance.

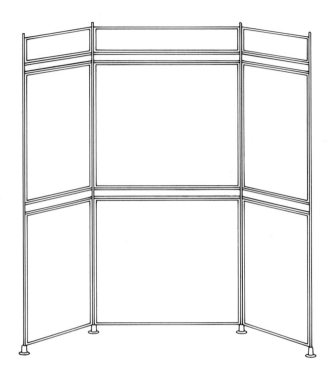

The benefits of the system are that it is reasonably flexible, quick and simple to erect and dismantle and easy to transport.

Larger systems

These are the true kit systems comprising individual panels which are fixed together using connectors. The bigger manufacturers provide a very wide range of different panels which can be put together in a multitude of different ways.

These systems are very flexible. You can start

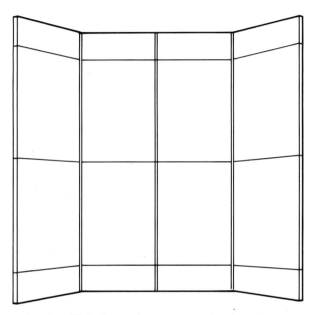

with a handful of panels to create a back wall, then by adding to the system you can grow it into a full scale exhibition system with cupboards, shelves, offices etc. When considering a system of this nature it is better to choose one from an established company so that you can ensure continuity of supply.

Buying an exhibition system

It is definitely worth buying a system from one of the established manufacturers especially if you are considering expanding the system or using it over a number of years. If the stand is to be put up by a number of different people then it is worth buying the simplest system you can find. Additionally

choose one with the fewest number of small bits, which tend to get lost and are normally very expensive to replace.

If appropriate choose a display system which can be used in a number of ways. You may be able to use the stand not only at exhibitions but also at the annual conference and possibly at smaller events.

When buying a system remember that the cost of the graphics, the bit which sells your company and it's products, may be as much as the system itself. As we said earlier it is the graphics which are going to do the selling not the system.

Another popular form of exhibiting is to organise your own event. Many organisations find that conventional exhibitions either fail to attract their target customers or that there are simply too few exhibitions to meet their marketing needs. The decision is therefore taken to organise a road-show, seminar, conference or open day.

In essence the rules which apply to exhibiting are the same as that for one of these activities except that you have to organise the venue and more importantly you are totally responsible for getting the visitors to attend. If you feel that to organise such an event will stretch the resources of your company too far then you can always employ an events company to organise it for you.

The principle benefits of organising your own event are that you:
● Choose the venue and timing of the event.
● You select the potential audience.

● Once you have got the visitor to attend you have no competition to worry about.

● You can control the size of the event and consequently spend the optimum time with each visitor.

Choosing the type of event

There are many different options to choose from. I have listed below the most common with a brief analysis of the benefits and disadvantages of each.

Road shows and other events

Here you are taking out your products or services to a series of events where you have the ability to show your customers the range which you are selling. If you have a wide range of products and one of your key objectives is to increase the number of products which your existing customers buy from you then a road-show can be a very effective way of doing this. The aim being to set up your shop near to your customers so that they can come and see the products you have on offer. You additionally have the opportunity of inviting potential customers to your road-shows and you have your technical staff available to provide technical support at the event.

Seminars and conferences

This is an extension of the Road-show where not only are you showing your products but you are also giving the visitor a presentation about the service or products which you supply. The main attraction for the visitor is that they are getting some technical training and therefore there is a better chance that the visitor will attend. It is worth charging a small fee for attending the seminar because once a person has parted with his money he is more likely to attend.

We currently run a seminar called a *A Guide to Better Exhibiting* at the Marler Haley Road-shows. Marler Haley is the leading manufacturer and supplier of exhibition systems in the UK and they hold road-shows around the country. They invite their existing customers and potential customers to attend the road-show and offer them the opportunity to attend the seminar.

The response to these events has been very good. Visitors not only gets an opportunity to see the different Marler Haley systems and talk to their senior design team, but they also get an opportunity of attending a seminar which hopefully they find helpful in maximising their future exhibition attendance.

Open days

The basic concept is to open up your factory, office, warehouse and invite your customers along to see your products or to learn about your services. These events can be particularly good if you have a site which is close to your customers. It does not necessarily have to be your own site. I once organised an Open day on a farm for Unigate's domestic customers.

The basic aim was as a public relations exercise. We invited the customers in East London to visit a farm in Epping. The day was billed as a free day out on the farm. Free parking, free entry, free Punch and Judy and free picnic area. The event was fantastically successful with thousands of very happy customers who were shown around a farm and shown how milk was produced. The company additionally covered it's costs by selling products at the open day.

As mentioned earlier in this book, not everyone is exhibiting with the aim of selling a product or service. Many organisations use exhibitions as a method for communicating messages and ideas. Open days can be used extremely effectively to achieve these particular aims.

Organising your own event

We have produced below a number of lists which are aimed at helping you to organise your own custom-built event.

Choosing the venue

The key decision is that the event should be held at the most convenient place possible. While in industry it is often acceptable to expect your visitors to travel by car for public shows you may need to be close to public transport. It is very important that the venue is appropriate to your company and the products or services you are trying to sell. It should neither be too up-market nor too down market for your potential customers. Always visit the venue before booking it. The key questions you are likely to want answered are:

- Parking facilities
- Disabled facilities
- What other events are going on at the same time
- Total numbers which can be accommodated
- Catering facilities
- Accommodation/special rates for your staff and visitors
- Presentation facilities

Timing of the event

I suspect more events fail because of poor timing than for any other reason. You need to choose a date and time for the event which does not coincide with other activities which your potential visitors may be interested in. Mondays and Fridays are usually avoided in the belief that the visitor does not want to travel on these days.

Weeks with bank holidays in them are often avoided because there may be a lot of people on holiday. August is often avoided for the same reason and of course the second half of December and Easter tend to be inappropriate times.

If you are running a day's seminar then it is worth remember that there will always be the odd delegate who turns up late. I normally recommend a 9.30am start with the expectation of actually starting at nearer 10.00am. Equally for seminars it is worth finishing at around 4.00pm. I am always amazed by the number of delegates who feel the need to get away early.

With evening events then you may like to consider provide transport home at the end of the event to make the whole package that bit more attractive.

Marketing the event

When buying space at an exhibition you are doing so because the organiser has given you some expectation of the number of people who are going to attend. When running your own event you need to generate your own visitors. Therefore the marketing of the event becomes one of the most important aspects. Having chosen your venue you need to decide the optimum number of visitors and plan your marketing accordingly.

Normally this will involve sending out invitations to existing and potential customers. This invitation needs to include some method by which the visitor registers that he will be attending the event. When we organised the Unigate Open-days we sent out leaflets outlining the event and asked customers to apply for tickets, stating clearly that the event was ticket only.

This at least gave us some measure of the people that were likely to attend the event. If you are providing refreshments then you need to have a very clear idea about the numbers attending. It may be worth considering making a small charge to cover this particular cost.

Timing of your marketing is also very important. In some industries people are booked up for four weeks ahead and therefore the invitation needs to be sent well in advance of this. In other industries it may be appropriate to give less notice.

If you are looking to attract new customers to your event then you will need to advertise the event in different ways. -in publications, purchasing mailing lists, advertising on the television or radio.

Ensure that you brief your salesforce well in advance of the event as they can tell their existing customers about it and encourage them to come.

Event preparation

As you are responsible for all aspects of the event you need to give particular attention to preparing preparation. You will probably require access to the venue the day before so that you can set up your displays and dry run your presentations etc. On average it takes four times longer to set up an event than it does to clear up afterwards. Always allow extra time during the set up to allow for those unforeseen hiccoughs.

If you are running a presentation or seminar then you need to consider if the participants will need desks in front of them to write on and indeed the material that you will be giving them to take away with them.

Signage at the event, especially at some of the large venues, can be important. If you are expecting thousands of people then consider getting an organisation like the AA or RAC to arrange roadsigns. This will be appropriate if the venue is difficult to find.

Refreshments during an event such as this are one of the items that your visitors are most likely to complain about. It is worth checking carefully with the caterers how, when and where the refreshments are to be served. Prepare a time schedule for them so that there is a chance that they will stick to it. Put one of your staff in charge of this aspect so that it is managed during the day.

Cloakroom facilities are also a consideration.

Public relations
As with ordinary exhibitions the opportunity exists for good PR during the event. Make sure that you invite the relevant press and that you send out details of the event both before, during and after. Treat your event in exactly the same way as you would for a standard exhibition and you should get very good press coverage.

Follow-up after the event
In exactly the same way as a normal exhibition you need to have planned your follow-up in advance of the event. Remember that the follow-up is in practice the fulfilment of the promises your staff make during the day. In order to turn interest in to future orders you need to follow-up effectively afterwards

Evaluation
Having run the event and hopefully had a busy day you need to review this marketing activity carefully afterwards. By doing so you will be better able to judge if it is a worthwhile form of marketing and consequently plan future events better.

Summary
- Small exhibitors do not always to book shell-scheme
- Make an impact by trying to be different
- Use a system stand that you can transport eas-ily
- Modular stands are usually just a backdrop.
- Consider what you really have to display
- Re-read the chapter on graphics *(page 32)*
- By putting your exhibition on the road, you can reach a highly selected audience
- Remember that you are totally responsible for inviting visitors
- Attract people by offering a varied, interesting and new programme
- Thorough planning is the key to a smooth operation

This section deals with all those people who believe that they have nothing to sell. This attitude is quite understandable. There are many people who go to exhibitions with just an idea or a message: no goods or money change hands, no service is rendered, no business is conducted. Unfortunately these stands tend to be rather dull and boring and we can only guess that this is for two reasons.

1. Because they are not driven by commercial gain, these type of stands are far less focussed on any particular aims.

2. The people running these stands are not so aware of how to promote or publicise their message.

We would like to address how we can tackle both of these problems.

Which stands?

At most trade and public exhibitions there are stands taken by organisations concerned with standards, safety, public information or membership. For example:
● A stand promoting road safety or driving standards.
● The Citizens Advice Bureau showing the extent of their work.
● The Benefits Agency showing what financial help is available.
● The U.K. Passport Agency offering advice on passport matters.
● Health and Safety Executive with information and advice.
● A Local Authority with a wide variety of information about their activities.
● Professional or trade bodies who set and uphold standards.
● The local police force who display their activities at open days or County Shows.
● Clubs and societies looking for new members.
● Magazines and journals promoting readership.
● Environmental or political pressure groups, or other campaigners.

The common feature about all these people is that they have nothing to 'sell' in the original sense of the word. If you asked many people on these stands, they would have no fixed ideas about what their aims were or whether the exhibition was successful for them. For those that do talk about their aims, I invariably hear that they wish to 'spread the word' or just 'let everyone know what we do'. This is all too imprecise, undefined, unmeasurable, unspecific and floppy.

Sell ... The 'S-word'

We have mentioned elsewhere in the book that we ought to take a very broad attitude to this word 'sell'. Many people do not like to sell, or even think

that what they are doing is selling, because they do not wish to appear pushy. Other people dislike the thought of selling because of the fear of rejection. Others dislike selling because they are just lazy. Whatever the reason, some people believe that they are not on an exhibition stand to sell anything. So how can we better define the word? How about:
1. To find out who may need what you have got.
2. To offer it to them.
3. To record whether they accept your offer.

This may be a very low key selling approach, but it is perhaps better suited to those without commercial objects to sell.

Setting aims
The above formula may help you formulate what your aims are for going to a show; for example, who are you trying to speak to? And what do you want to tell them? You should try to be specific. If you are an organisation looking for new members, then instead of saying: "we would like to attract whoever is interested in our society," you could say: "we want to show the benefits of membership to fifty local self-employed business people from central Manchester." These are specific and quantifiable targets.

If you are a road safety organisation then maybe your aims could be to talk to fifty car drivers and fifty children under ten and offer them some information on your subject. Whatever your aims are they must somehow be pro-active, that is to say they must include an activity that will involve you in doing something more than waiting for people to come to you.

What exactly are you offering?
Okay, so you are not going to the show to sell nuts, bolts and widgets. But why exactly are you going? Or, at worst, what have you got to give away? A leaflet? An application form? An information sheet? Can you make that information take on some value? Can you sell it for free and for nothing? The way to go about this is to use the Positive Professional Approach. This involves a great deal of filtering of the visitors to the show to find the ones who may be a potential target for your message. For example, first of all approach all the people passing your stand with a couple of closed questions; "Excuse me sir, are you a car driver?" "Excuse me madam, are you a reader of *Spot-Welding Monthly*?" "Excuse me, we're doing a survey of users of the local Leisure Centre..." After this, you can at least offer your information to a selected audience, which gives it some added value. It also means that you can record your successes i.e. start to measure the information given, or the conversations had, against your aims for going to the show.

What should you record?
If you stand on the edge of the gangway and give out leaflets to every passer by, you may as well count the hairs in the palm of your hand. But if you can count 'qualified' visitors i.e. those who have

already expressed an interest in your message, then you are already counting sales. By doing this, you are creating a measure for whether you have achieved your aims. In turn, this will help you assess whether your attendance at the show was worthwhile. One company we know who offer vocational training courses, recorded every leaflet that was taken away from their stand by potential students, parents and employers. By doing this they worked out that exhibitions were a far more effective form of publicity than any form of magazine advertising.

Selling the message

Perhaps one of the greatest failures of most stands who have a message to sell is that they fail completely to put that message on their stand. It is not sufficient just to put up the name of your organisation and to assume that visitors will know either who you are or what you are doing there. As with all graphics, keep your message bold, brief and simple. Here are a few examples based on the organisations mentioned earlier:

How to Prevent Accidents on the Roads...
A Range of Advice for Almost Every Situation
Information on Your Rights To Claim
Help With Your Passport Application
Information On Activities in Your Area
Free Health and Safety Advice
New Members Welcome
Free Trial Subscription
Ten Simple Ways To Help Your Local

Environment
Now, none of these are particularly inspired but they are already one hundred percent better than nothing and nothing is what I normally see on exhibition stands of this nature. If you have a message to sell, remember to sell it!

Selling benefits, not features

The problem with selling messages and not products or services is that it is very easy to fall in to the trap of selling features not benefits. A simple example of this is the Road Safety stand where the stand staff are liable to tell the visitors that it is now law to wear seat belts in the back of cars if the car is fitted with them. Most people do not like wearing seat-belts as they find them restricting. By selling the feature, the fact, that you now have to wear seat-belts will be an uphill struggle for the stand staff.

The benefit on the other hand is that by wearing a seat-belt you are much less likely to be seriously injured if you have an accident. As most people do not want to be injured the sales message how not to get injured is much more appealing than the law that you have to wear a seat-belt.

Every feature of your message can be turned in to a benefit. A good way of developing a list of benefits is to get the stand staff to draw up a list of the features of your message and then working as a group to produce the benefits. By doing this the stand staff are much more likely to sell the benefits when working on the exhibition stand.

Summary

- Even if you are only giving advice then you need to 'sell'.
- Set aims so that you have something to measure your performance against.
- Sell the benefits not the features of your advice.